THE
MONOPOLY®
BOOK

THE

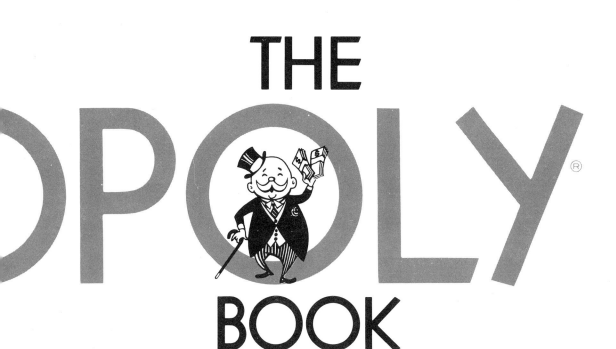

OPOLY®

BOOK

Strategy and Tactics
of the World's Most Popular Game

MAXINE BRADY

David McKay Company, Inc., New York

For Frank, without whom it would
not have been

The Monopoly® Book
Copyright ©1974 by Maxine Brady

ISBN: 0-679-20292-7
Library of Congress Catalog Card Number: 74-6748
Manufactured in the United States of America

Designed by Gene Siegel

Third Printing, November 1974

Acknowledgments

Many people offered me their time, advice, and assistance as I was researching and writing this book. Mike Alber must get my special thanks for allowing me to pore over his voluminous files, helping me unearth obscure facts, and for patiently bearing with me as I raised question after question about the rules of the game in my effort to explain and clarify them. Randolph and Robert B. M. Barton kindly searched their memories to recall the precise circumstances of Parker Brothers' earliest experiences with Monopoly, and Mrs. Esther Darrow was good enough to provide her own recollections of her husband's invention of and early adventures with the game.

Andrea Donahue, Maria D'Iorio, and June Butcher spent time digging into Parker Brothers' archives to examine early versions of Monopoly. They also provided me with many of the questions that confuse Monopoly players, which I have tried to answer in this book. Lee Weisenthal generously gave me much of his valuable time to provide information on tournament Monopoly.

I would like to give special thanks to Wallace Exman, my editor, whose enthusiasm, advice, foresight, and good cheer made our work together a pleasure.

To Frank, for his hilarious inspirations, to Larry and Sue Waldman for their help with some of the charts and tables, to Lisa and Stuart Isacoff, Irma Heldman, Steve Cutler, Spencer, Marion, Bill, Marsha, Laurie, Bill, Ann, Susan, Neil and all the many Monopoly buffs whose laughter, screams, joys, frustrations, giggles, and gnashings helped me to understand something about the mind of the Monopoly player, thank you. May you each win second prize in a beauty contest.

Contents

Preface   9

1. Monopolia Curiosa   13

In the Beginning, There Was the Great Depression   14

Yes, Virginia, There Is an Atlantic City   21

Upside Down and Under Water?   24

What Do You Mean, "Play Money"?   29

Here, There, and Just About Everywhere   30

What? *That* Old Game?   32

2. Understanding the Rules   35

The Object of the Game   37

The Players   37

Preparing the Cards   38

The Banker   38

The Bank   38

Buildings   39

Chance and Community Chest   39

Buying and Trading Property   47

Buying Buildings   50

Building Shortage   55

Rent   57

Mortgaging   61

Selling Buildings   64

Jail   70

GO   72

Income Tax   73

Free Parking   74

Bankruptcy   75

Variations   77

The Free Parking Jackpot   78

Maximum Punishment   78

GO to GO   79

Doubling Up   79

Immunity   79

Short Monopoly   81

3. Strategy and Tactics   83

Basic Principles   84

How to Decide Which Property Group to Develop   87

How Many Buildings?   91

The Facts of Probability   92

Special Strategies and Tactics   94

The Prince or the Pauper   94

The Pauper's Attack   95

The Prince's Restraint   98

The Money Method   100

The Premature Development Risk   101

The Monetary Bluff   102

The Midas Mistake   103

The Bidder's Delight   104

The Railroad Offensive   105
The Utilities Folly   107
The Building Formation   108
The Construction Gambit   110
The Edifice Complex   112
The Mortgage Morass   114
The Profitable Loss   117
The Beggar's Offense   119
The Pecuniary Plunge   119
The Bankruptcy Deferred   120
Beat the Cheat   122
Epilogue: How to Deal with Tantrums   125
Appendix   128
Property Development Tables   128
Property Desirability Index   137
Parker Brothers Official Monopoly Rules   139

Preface

I have never witnessed a quiet Monopoly game. No matter who the opponents, or how old, or how extensive or nonexistent their real-world assets, as soon as people sit down to play this game, at least mild pandemonium is sure to ensue. In part, this is caused by the very nature of the game. Monopoly brings out a fierce competitive instinct, even in normally mild mannered people. Perhaps the compulsion to acquire wealth and possessions is an unheralded instinct.

Undoubtedly, though, much of the uproar that accompanies each game occurs as contestants dispute the rules. And this is rather strange. Monopoly is not very hard to understand or to learn to play, and most of the loudest disputes are between players who have known the game for years. Why is there so much confusion?

It seems that Monopoly has become almost a part of our folk heritage. It has been around since 1934, so many of today's adults learned the game as children. They use their sets year after year, passing them on to their children as a kind of cultural heirloom. "Here's the family Monopoly set, Mary. Take care of it. Use it well." But by now the Old Set is a bit timeworn. The Chance and Community Chest cards are faded and dog-eared. The money is limp and crumpled; many of the bills are held together with Scotch tape. There's a token missing; it has been replaced by a pale red checker. And the original rules were lost long ago.

None of this dampens anyone's enthusiasm. Sooner or later, the mood will strike. For the aficionado, all that is necessary are a few uninterrupted hours. For the "former" player, it may be a particular rainy, miserable afternoon, or a night when there's simply *nothing* on television. But sooner or later, someone will make the suggestion, Let's play Monopoly.

So who rereads the rules? Do you ever forget how to ride a bicycle? You just clear off the table or floor, sit down around the board, argue a bit about how to dispense the money, and start to play.

And therein lies part of the reason for this book. Over and over I've heard the plaintive cry, "That's not the way *we* used to play." People seem to remember the most fascinating, and creative, points of order:

The money from Income Tax gets put under Free Parking . . .

When you're in Jail, you can't collect rent on your properties . . .

You can't buy any property until you've gone around the board at least once . . .

If you land on GO you collect $400 . . .

Many of these "house rules" appear more common than the rules that Parker Brothers includes in each set. Hardly anyone I've spoken to, for instance, was unaware of the "rule" of putting the money from taxes and fines under Free Parking, to be "won" by the player lucky enough to land on that square. And that's the way I remember playing, too. But the rules are very clear if one takes the time to read them: "A player landing on this space [Free Parking] does not receive any money, property or reward of any kind. This is just a 'free' resting place."

How could that be? Has Parker Brothers gone and changed the rules on us? Amazingly, they haven't. The rules for Monopoly, like the design of the board, are essentially the same today as they were when Charles Darrow invented the game. The problem is twofold: first, many people rely on memory, and memory can be faulty. We misremember certain rules, and played with agreed-upon house rules which we now recall as an intrinsic part of the game. Secondly, the printed rules are sometimes sadly unclear and ambiguous, even for players who are trying to play by the book.

One of the principal functions of this book is to explain and clarify those rules, to preserve the sanctity of families and friendships, and to avoid some of the obstacles that get in the way of just playing Monopoly. I have also attempted to catalog some of the many strategies that operate during a good game, but which most players seem unconscious of, even when they themselves are using the strategies to excellent advantage. Monopoly is *not* merely a game of chance. There are definite techniques by which you can improve your chances of winning.

Researching the history of the game was a bit like tiptoeing through a penny candy store, nose pressed against the glass counters. The chronicle of Monopoly provides a nostalgic view of a facet of America, and the game's personal statistics are awesome. (For instance, since first entering this nether world of pseudo real estate, Parker Brothers has constructed 2,560,000,000 of those little green houses.)

But for some reason, the game seems to lend itself to believe-it-or-not type fads. Swallowing live goldfish is nothing when compared with the amazing antics of Monopoly players. I have tried to capture some of the irrepressible zaniness of the game, which causes otherwise rational people to do the most incredible things. I still don't quite know why.

M.B.

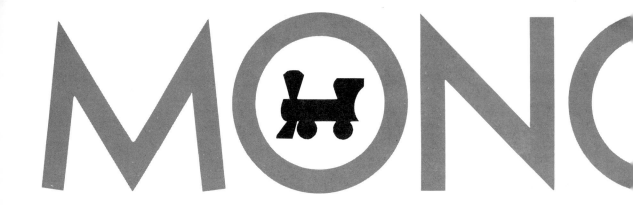

1
Monopolia
Curiosa

In the Beginning, There Was the Great Depression

The stock market crash of 1929 caused mass unemployment for millions of Americans. For Charles Darrow, the financial problems grew increasingly difficult. Once a salesman of heating and engineering equipment, he spent the early 1930s looking for a job. He'd been feeding himself, his wife, and their son by taking any odd job he could find. He repaired electric irons, did occasional fix-it jobs, even walked dogs—when he could find someone to pay him for his labors.

It wasn't enough, though. Now his wife was expecting their second child. He had to find a way to make more money.

To fill his many idle hours, and help him forget his worries temporarily, Darrow invented things. Some of them were fun; others were probably devised in hopes that they would become profitable. He made jigsaw puzzles; he created a combination bat-and-ball, which was supposed to be used as a beach toy; he designed an improved pad for recording and scoring bridge games. They were interesting diversions, but nobody was willing to pay for them.

Darrow's problem, of course, was not unique. Many of his friends and family were out of jobs, and were having trouble affording even such necessities as food and shelter. For them, as for most people, the movies, the theater, and any form of entertainment which cost any money at all was too expensive.

So they got together in the evenings and on weekends, when the offices of the Federal Emergency Relief Administration were closed, and they talked. And after the gloomy recital of that day's particular troubles, the conversation would usually become nostalgic: remember the good old days?

Darrow did. For him and his wife, thinking back to the more prosperous life they had led only a few years before, some of the pleasantest memories were of the vacations they had spent at one of their favorite holiday places, a seaside resort in New Jersey called Atlantic City.

One evening in 1930, Darrow sat down at his kitchen table in Germantown, Pennsylvania, and sketched out some of the street names of Atlantic City on the round piece of oilcloth that covered the table. The streets he chose were all from the same side of the city: between the Inlet and Park Place, along the Boardwalk. When he finished, Darrow was short one name, so he choose Marven Gardens, a section from nearby Margate. Probably unintentionally, he altered the spelling, and it was penciled onto his board as Marvin Gardens.

He included the three railroads that carried the wealthy vacationers to the resort, and the utility companies that serviced them, as well as the parcels of real estate of varying prices. He wanted a fourth railroad to make his board symmetrical, so he added the Short Line: actually it was a freight-carrying bus company that had a depot in Atlantic City. A local paint store gave him free samples of several colors, and he used them to color his game board. A new game began to take form in his mind.

Darrow cut houses and hotels for his little city, using scraps of wooden molding that a lumber yard had discarded. He rounded up stray pieces of cardboard, and typed out title cards for the different properties. The rest of the equipment was fairly easy to acquire: colored buttons for the tokens, a pair of dice, and a lot of play money.

From then on, in the evenings, the Darrows would sit around the kitchen table buying, renting, developing, and selling real estate. They had little enough real cash on hand, yet The Game, as they all referred to it, permitted them to manipulate large sums of money as they engaged in complex negotiations to acquire valuable blocks of property. The simple, almost crude set exerted a continuing fascination and challenge. As friends dropped in to visit, they were invited to join the game. Soon the "Monopoly evenings" became a standard feature at the Darrow home.

Then the friends wanted to take the game home with them. Each night's winner, a bit heady with his success in the nether reaches of high finance, asked for a set of his own, so that he could show off his financial wizardry. The runner-up, convinced that he could win the next time if he could only hone his skill with a little practice, generally wanted a set too. Darrow had

15

an overabundance of free time, so he began making copies of his board, property cards, and buildings. His delighted friends supplied their own dice and tokens, and often their own package of play money.

But the demand increased, and Darrow increased his output to two hand-made sets a day. Selling them for $4 apiece, each set brought him new customers. People kept talking about the new game and playing it with their friends. Through word-of-mouth advertising alone, Darrow sold about one hundred sets, and had orders for many more. But his one-at-a-time production technique simply couldn't keep up with the demand.

Encouraged by his friends, Darrow decided to test the game outside his personal sphere of acquaintances and friends of friends. He made up a few sets and offered them to department stores in Philadelphia, the nearest city. They sold.

With the knowledge that his game was marketable, he attempted to increase his rate of production. A friend helped out by printing the Monopoly boards and the title cards. Darrow continued to paint in the colors and assemble the sets by hand. This partial automation enabled him to produce six games a day. It wasn't enough.

By 1934, now fully aware that his interesting diversion had turned into a potentially profitable business, Darrow arranged to have the same friend print and package the complete sets. It looked like they had the problem solved, for a little while. Production was finally keeping pace with sales. But they hadn't reckoned with the Philadelphia sales. Soon, a department store began ordering sets wholesale, in quantities far greater than anything they could accommodate. It became obvious to Darrow that he had only two choices. He could borrow money and plunge wholeheartedly into the game business, or he could sell Monopoly to an established game company. Darrow wrote to Parker Brothers, then as now one of the world's major game manufacturers and distributors, to see if the company would be interested in producing and marketing the game on a national basis.

Parker Brothers had by then been in business for half a century, and had become accustomed to enthusiastic inventors sending in new game creations. Some of the ideas had even proven marketable, but, by and large, the company's managers tended to trust the creativity of their own staff far more than they did an unproven novice.

Although Parker Brothers thought the basic framework of the game seemed possibly interesting, they handled the game routinely. Various members of the company sat down at their offices in Salem, Massachusetts, to try it out, as they do all prospective games. They played it several times and found that they all enjoyed it. But the company had evolved a set of inviolable ground rules for "family games," which they held to be mandatory for any game that could be successfully marketed. According to the Parker precept, a family game should last approximately forty-five minutes. Monopoly could go on for hours. Parker also felt that a game should have a specific end, a goal to be achieved. (In their other board games, the players' tokens progressed around a track until they reached the end—which might be symbolized by a pot of gold, a home port, a jackpot, or even Heaven—and the first player to reach this goal was the winner.) In Monopoly, the players just kept going round and round the board. The only goal was to bankrupt the other players and emerge still solvent yourself. Furthermore, Monopoly's rules seemed far too complex to the Parker staff; they thought the general game-playing public would be hopelessly confused trying to learn how to handle mortgages, rents, and interest.

After testing the game for several weeks, Parker Brothers made the unanimous decision to reject it. The company wrote and informed Darrow of this decision, explaining that his game contained "fifty-two fundamental errors." It would never be accepted by the public.

Darrow, of course, was considerably annoyed. He knew very well how people responded to his game. Despite Parker Brothers' analysis, Monopoly was decidedly marketable. Unfortunately, however, it was far more marketable than Darrow himself; he was still unemployed. Monopoly, it seemed, was virtually his only asset.

Therefore, he went back to his printer friend, ordered the production of five thousand sets, and continued to sell the game locally. But locally included Philadelphia, and the department stores there were soon aware that Darrow was increasing his output. They began placing massive orders for the Christmas season. Darrow now found himself working fourteen hours a day just trying to keep up with the shipping.

With the game now being ordered in wholesale lots, Parker's sales representatives soon became acutely aware that the Philadelphia stores were expecting huge sales of Monopoly the following Christmas, the traditional game-buying season. Word was quickly passed back to corporate headquarters in Salem, where the issue was deemed worthy of reconsideration. Then, to top things off, a major New York toy and game store, the prestigious F. A. O. Schwarz, bought two hundred sets out of the original five thousand printing.

Shortly afterwards, a friend telephoned Sally Barton (daughter of Parker Brothers' founder, George Parker) to rave about a wonderful new game she had purchased at F. A. O. Schwarz. It was called Monopoly, and it was hard to come by and in short supply. The friend suggested that Mrs. Barton tell Parker Brothers about it. Sally did. She told her husband, Robert B. M. Barton, who happened to be the president of the company. Curious about a competitor's product, he purchased a copy of the game at F. A. O. Schwarz, took it home and wound up playing it until 1 A.M. The next day, Barton wrote to Darrow, and three days later they met at Parker Brothers' New York sales office in the Flatiron Building.

Parker Brothers offered to buy the game outright and give Darrow royalties on all sets sold. The company insisted, though, on making some revisions which would refine the game and clarify the rules. Some of the staff were still concerned about the indefinite playing time, so they agreed to market the original version as long as Darrow permitted them to develop a variation of the game which could be played in less time. This shorter version was to be printed along with the general rules, to give the public an option.

Darrow agreed and the contract was signed. Later, in explaining why he had decided to sell his brainchild, Darrow related his decision to the monetary commitment he would have otherwise had to make in order to keep producing the game himself. "Taking the precepts of Monopoly to heart," he said, "I did not care to speculate." Years afterward, commenting on the final offer from Parker Brothers, he wrote: "I gladly accepted and have never regretted that decision."

The royalties from sales of Monopoly soon made Darrow a millionaire. He retired at the age of forty-six, to become a gentleman farmer in Bucks County, Pennsylvania, a world traveler with a particular interest in ancient cities, a motion picture photographer, and a collector of exotic orchid species. In 1970, a few years after Darrow's death, Atlantic City erected a commemorative plaque in his honor. It stands on the Boardwalk, near the juncture of Park Place.

Meanwhile, Parker Brothers still had the problem of coping with this incredible new acquisition. For all of their years of game experience, the staff had never seen anything like the phenomenon of Monopoly.

The comparatively small number of sets which had been sold by Darrow had done their work in arousing the public to an awareness of the fascinating new game. People who had a set played it frequently, thus introducing Monopoly to new converts, who then wanted sets of their own. When word got out in early 1935 that Darrow had sold his game to Parker Brothers, people began writing to the company, asking to buy sets.

The company's normally quiet offices in Salem became a bedlam of back orders. The letters and telegraphed requests completely overwhelmed the order department, which couldn't even find space for all the pieces of correspondence. In desperation, the company brought in large laundry baskets and filled them with unprocessed orders. The baskets lined the hallways, getting in everyone's way as the company worked feverishly to produce and ship the required number of sets. And still the orders flooded in.

As Christmas neared, the delighted officials realized that their much over-worked staff needed help. They contacted a large bookkeeping firm in Boston, but when the firm's representatives got to Salem, they took one look at the chaos and refused to take the job.

Somehow, the orders were filled and Parker Brothers, now producing more than 20,000 sets a week, were able to keep up with the demand. By the end of the first year of marketing Monopoly on a national level, while the country was still in the midst of a depression, Parker had sold more than one million sets—an unheard-of phenomenon.

But it couldn't be expected to continue. Once before, Parker Brothers had overproduced and overstocked a game, and the results had been nearly disastrous. In 1924, the Oriental game of Mah-Jongg had been imported into the United States and had swept the country. The sets of ivory tiles and bamboo (later plastic) rods for counting chips sold for anywhere from a few dollars to over $150, and the game quickly became a fad, complete with Oriental costumes, furniture, and accessories. Then, in 1929, quite suddenly and unexpectedly, the market for Mah-Jongg collapsed, along with the stock market. Parker Brothers was left with hundreds of expensive sets in the warehouse.

Doubtless afraid of repeating the error, George S. Parker, founder and then Chairman of the Board of the company, decided to cease production of Monopoly. He and his staff expected that the game would sell well for a total of about three years, and then the public would lose interest in the novelty. They thought, too, that their buyers would be adults, since the game seemed to be too difficult for children. And, by late 1936, sales had begun to level off, as predicted.

On December 19, 1936, George Parker sent an inter-office memo, ordering the company to "cease absolutely to make any more boards or utensil boxes" because ". . . we will stop making any Monopoly against the possibility of a very early slump." His memo, however, was written just before Christmas, the traditional game-buying season. As sets were exchanged and played with, the interest in the game rose again—and this time, it had a new audience. Children had learned to play from their parents, and now they wanted their own sets.

At that point, Parker Brothers' management acknowledged that they could not make any predictions about Monopoly. The game simply refused to obey any of the traditional rules. So they quietly resumed production, and Monopoly quietly resumed selling, happily unaware of its fifty-two fundamental errors. It has been a bestseller every year since it came out, and by the end of 1974 it had sold almost eighty million sets.

Yes, Virginia, There is an Atlantic City

There is no truth to the rumor that the founding fathers of Atlantic City used a Monopoly board as a guide when they mapped the city. Atlantic City was incorporated in 1854. Monopoly was invented in 1933.

The first street map of Atlantic City was completed on December 25, 1852. The East–West streets were named for the seas, and the North–South streets were named for the states. Matters remained this way until 1973. Then progress, or the urge to become modern, nearly created a disaster. Arthur W. Ponzio, the Commissioner of Public Works of Atlantic City, New Jersey, began to have visions of renewed glory for his city. Word was out that some major monied investors were considering turning Atlantic City into the Las Vegas of the East. This proposal would doubtless bring renewed capital into the city's dwindling economy.

Mr. Ponzio thought the city needed a major upgrading. As part of his city beautification, Ponzio proposed that the City Commission change the names of Baltic and Mediterranean Avenues.

It seems that there is indeed some confusion on the Atlantic City street maps with regard to these two avenues. Baltic Avenue, for instance, is one of three names given to the same street as it meanders across town. Mr. Ponzio argued that tourists were confused by the change of name. In an effort to create order and ease the minds of tourists, he decided to use one of the three names, Fairmont, for the entire street.

Mediterranean Avenue is one of two names given to another street, and the commissioner chose to use the alternate name, Melrose Avenue, for that entire street. The two streets, now bearing single names for their entire lengths, were then each to be made one way, in keeping with the modernization and "upgrading" plan. In reality, both Baltic and Mediterranean Avenues in Atlantic City are less than picturesque streets. It is symbolically appropriate that they are the cheapest properties on the Monopoly board. The properties on the real life streets include run-down homes, some of them boarded up, 21 vacant lots, taverns, and a junkyard of old plumbing equipment. Baltic Avenue does have a hotel, but it would not be classified as luxurious.

Nonetheless—or perhaps partly because Mediterranean and Baltic were the poorest properties on a Monopoly board—the proposal to change the street names caused virtual pandemonium. What would otherwise have remained a local city matter expanded outward to Monopoly players all across the continent. Virtually every Monopoly player, or everyone who remembered Monopoly with nostalgia, objected to the proposed name change. An avalanche of protests descended upon the amazed Atlantic City commissioners. On January 11, 1973, the city commission met to vote on the issue. Nearly three hundred people, newsmen and spectators, crowded into the hearing room to witness the historic dispute. The spectators overflowed into the corridor of the normally quiet building.

The two small streets had numerous champions to defend their existence. From prestigious Princeton University came the SSBMA (Students to Save Baltic and Mediterranean Avenues); their president and founder, Robert W. Baker, saw the issue as one of great social significance.

"The streets of Atlantic City, through the medium of Monopoly, have been a microcosm of life in which Baltic and Mediterranean have represented the last resort of the underdog to hold out against the oppressive forces of Boardwalk and Park Place powermongers."

Barry P. Waldman, associate general counsel of the USMA, which conducts the annual Midwest Regional Men's Invitational Monopoly Tournament, was an eloquent speaker who had flown in from Detroit specifically for this meeting of the city council. He called Baltic and Mediterranean Avenues "two national monuments," and told the commissioners that his organization had already asked the U.S. Department of Interior to block any action to change the street names. Randolph P. Barton, then executive vice-president of Parker Brothers, also flew to the site of contention to speak before the commission. In his eloquent summation, Mr. Barton pointed out: "Millions of people look forward to passing GO, collecting $200, and landing on Mediterranean and Baltic Avenues."

Some city officials became embarrassed over the controversy and its implications that they were anti-American. Mayor Joseph F. Bradway, Jr. was careful to impress reporters with the fact that he was not personally against Monopoly. Leading the way into his private quarters, he proudly displayed a Monopoly rug, which held a place of honor on his bathroom floor.

Parker Brothers made the firm decision to retain the historic names of Baltic and Mediterranean Avenues on their Monopoly boards regardless of the decision of the Atlantic City commissioners. The company felt that it would be doing "a disservice to both the game and this city to change these street names which have become a part of Americana." As Mr. Barton pointed out, strategic building of the Baltic–Mediterranean Avenue properties can sometimes be the winning factor in an otherwise tight game.

The commissioners listened to all of the arguments. They were also deeply impressed by a letter written to the commissioner of public works by Mr. Edward P. Parker, then president of Parker Brothers. Parker wrote in part:

> While I certainly agree with the logic of having a street name remain the same for its entire length, I feel that this is a special case whose repercussions could possibly shake the very foundations of American tradition—and in particular a tradition that has spanned four generations and brought fame and fortune to your fair city.
>
> The names "Baltic" and "Mediterranean" are not just local street names whose function is to locate different points in your city. These streets cannot be compared to Main Street or Elm Street in Anytown, U.S.A. They must be included in the category containing such thoroughfares as Broadway, Trafalgar Square, and the Champs Elysées. Who would ever suggest changing *their* names? Baltic and Mediterranean Avenues belong to America and to the Americans whose love of Monopoly has made them famous.
>
> Would you like to be the man to tell a Monopoly fanatic from California that the streets he came to see no longer exist? Would you be willing to take the responsibility for an invasion by

hordes of protesting Monopoly players, all demanding that you go directly to jail, without even the dignity of passing GO?

Mr. Parker's protests accurately indicated that the devotion to Monopoly was enormously widespread. In fact, the Atlantic City commission received a protest from a group of 250 Monopoly aficionados in London, Ontario, who protested vehemently against being deprived of "a little corner of America."

By this time, even Mr. Ponzio was unhappy with his suggestion. With none of the other commissioners favoring his proposal, the besieged Ponzio proposed that his own suggestion be vetoed, and the names of the streets left intact. A compromise solution was suggested by Mr. Waldman of the USMA. He advised that Baltic Avenue be extended to become the sole name of that street, and that Mediterranean Avenue be used as the sole name for its street. Mr. Ponzio conceded this to be a good idea, belatedly acknowledging that Mediterranean and Baltic Avenues "belong to America, to the people."

The public hearing at City Hall lasted just twenty minutes in the bright glare of the television cameras. The five-man commission unanimously agreed to accept Ponzio's proposal that his bill be killed. And when the voting was over, Commissioner Joseph Lazarow read the poem that he had written to express his feelings on this historic moment:

> To this ordinance vote no.
> To our residents it presents a great woe.
> Baltic and Mediterranean are the streets we know.
> Without them we could never pass GO.

Upside Down and Under Water?

There is something about Monopoly that evokes the spirits both of creativity and competition. Not content merely to build real estate empires, Monopoly buffs seem compelled to play their game in ways undreamed of by the late

Mr. Darrow. He played it in his kitchen. His hordes of disciples, most of whom do not know his name, play it in elevators, in bomb shelters, in airplanes, in pup tents, and in even more unlikely places and circumstances.

Playing it, of course, is not enough. Recognition for the truly fantastic, fascinating feats of Monopoly is justly sought, and so the Monopoly Marathon Records Documentation Committee was formed. Now chaired by Mike Alber, the committee today is headquartered at 509 Madison Avenue, New York, N.Y. 10022. It accepts and adjudicates Monopoly marathons in several established categories, and is open to suggestions because, inevitably, people think of yet another way in which Monopoly simply must be played.

Marathons originally consisted of a single game, stretched out for as many hours as possible. In order to prolong the game, players resorted to some rather radical techniques, generally involving the use of huge sums of Monopoly money.

If a player were about to go bankrupt, the Bank would suddenly issue a dividend: every player would receive a large cash bonus. This would suffice to keep the potential debtor in the game, but it caused a constant drain on the Bank's finances. Marathon Banks were perennially running out of money, and players telephoned or telegraphed Parker Brothers at all hours of the day or night to report the financial crisis and ask for additional funding. After one such request, which happened to occur at three A.M., the Monopoly Marathon Records Documentation Committee held a meeting with a panel of distinguished economists. Their joint decision has changed the playing habits of a host of contestants. No longer must a marathon be one continuous game. It may be a succession of games, played one after another: as soon as one game ends, the next game must begin. This new system seems to be working well. Mike Alber reports that he has been getting much more sleep, lately.

The first officially recognized Monopoly happening occurred in 1961, when a fraternity at the University of Pittsburgh played a 161–hour game. This original record was broken fifteen times until a group in Danville, California, finally ·awed all comers into respectful submission. Twenty people played in this non-stop marathon that began at noon on July 21, 1971 and stopped thirty-four days later, at 4 P.M. on August 24. The record stood for three years: 820 hours of continuous play. But Monopoly players are a dauntless lot. On June 18, 1974, at the apparently symbolic hour of noon, thirty-four students sat down in a Denver department store and announced that they intended to break the record. Playing in two-player, four-hour shifts, they ultimately lost track of the number of times they passed GO. A triumphant cheer was sounded by the intermittant onlookers as the 820–hour mark was passed, but the combatants were too engrossed in their trading at the moment to pay it much heed. Houses blended into hotels and the tokens wore a faint depression into the track they followed relentlessly round and round the board, but at noon on July 30, with TV cameras present to record the occasion, the ultimate goal was reached. One thousand and eight hours of continuous play. Forty-one nights. Forty-two days.

Naturally, besides this endurance record for the longest Monopoly game for an unlimited number of players, Monopoly records are maintained in various other specialized categories.

The largest outdoor game was played in 1967 by a group of students at Juniata College in Huntingdon, Pennsylvania. The game board, which measured 550′ x 470′, consisted of campus streets and sidewalks. The players relayed their moves to the living tokens, who were given their instructions by messengers on bicycles, who kept in touch with the players by walkie-talkie.

And then there was the largest indoor game, held in a shopping mall in Flint, Michigan, on June 10, 1972. The game board measured 52′ x 52′. Apparently the enormous size left normal mortals intimidated, for the participants of this spectacular were professional athletes. The winner, for the record, was Detroit Lions football player Lem Barney.

It must never be thought, though, that Monopoly marathons are confined to the province of professionals. Two teenage boys in Greeley, Colorado had once dug a 10′ x 4′ x 4′ hole in their backyard, for some now unimportant reason. The hole, actually more of a cave, sat unused for several years until one of the boys came up with a brilliant idea. The result was the world's record in underground Monopoly: a 100–hour game played in 1974 by eight Greeley teenagers. The boys were supplied with food (including popcorn), and other essentials during their ordeal, and were rewarded afterwards with a huge cake, baked and decorated by the sister of one of the participants. Reasonably enough, the cake was a perfect replica of a Monopoly board.

The world's first invitational antigravitational Monopoly game was held on April 10, 1974. The participants were two University of Michigan students, David Kemper and David Lichterman, who had drawn a 64 square foot board on the ceiling of their dormitory room with felt tip pens. To preserve their necks and their equilibrium, they played for only four hours.

An interesting problem developed during the testing of the antigravitational game. Obviously, the tokens supplied with the standard Monopoly wouldn't stay on the ceiling, so it was decided to use helium-filled balloons as moving pieces. Helium is not the easiest substance to find in Ann Arbor, so the contestants contacted Parker Brothers, who shipped in some canisters of the lighter-than-air gas. Balloons were, presumably, available.

A more difficult problem arose when a group of scuba divers from the Fidelity chapter of the Order of DeMolay, in Beverly, Massachusetts, decided to go for a new scuba record, using the pool at the New England Divers Club. They thought that playing Monopoly might be a good way to relieve underwater boredom. But the paper money, cards, and board tended to disintegrate after prolonged submersion.

A group of Parker Brothers engineers, who seem to be unusually cooperative about such things, worked for three weeks designing and creating—by hand—a special Monopoly set that could be used underwater. The resulting forty-two pound set was both waterproof and sinkable.

The actual components of the set were taken off the normal production line, and then customized. The plastic houses and hotels were hollowed out and filled with steel wool. The board label (the paper on which the playing area is printed) was laminated between several sheets of cellophane until it shone with a glass-like quality. Magnetic rubber strips were placed beneath it, and affixed to a quarter-inch steel plate. Now the board was both magnetic and heavy.

The property deed, Community Chest, and Chance cards were each laminated with a sheet of metal sandwiched in. At first, each of the 240 pieces of money was lacquered, but they fell apart after some use in the test tank. 27

Then the money was laminated with sheets of metal, but a stack of bills became too bulky for use. Ultimately, the money itself was simply laminated. It was waterproof, but the players had to exercise a bit of care to see that their cash didn't float away.

The DeMolay group set their record, but once word of the existence of the unique Monopoly set leaked out, enterprising scuba divers soon set out to break it. The current group record is held by another group of DeMolay fraternity members, who recently made additional history by playing in an outdoor pool, in Evansville, Indiana. The open setting caused a rather unique situation. Four divers entered the pool at midnight and remained submerged for thirty hours. Then a violent thunderstorm arose, and the group was forced to evacuate the pool for fifteen minutes until the threat of lightning had passed.

But how would that affect their official timing? No one knew, so the Monopoly Marathon Documentation Committee was contacted for a ruling. The Committee declared that the original thirty hours were forfeit, and timing must begin again when the team resubmerged. The good-natured divers accepted the verdict, swam down to their waiting dice, and did not emerge for another seventy-two hours. With the exception of their fifteen minutes on the surface, they were underwater more than one hundred hours. They also hold the distinction of playing in the first Monopoly tournament to be interrupted by an Act of God. Briefly.

Monopoly can have its ups and downs, though, and twelve people in Torrance, California, really proved the point. They played Monopoly in a moving elevator. For one hundred and forty-eight hours, they occupied a table in an elevator at the Holiday Inn, and parlayed properties as passengers kibitzed. And wondered.

It should be pointed out that once upon a time, the Monopoly Marathon Records Documentation Committee recognized the category of Two Player Monopoly. This consisted of two opponents, playing continuously, with no relief replacements, for as long as they could hold out. In 1972, however, the committee met in consultation with a panel of distinguished physicians, and decided that they would no longer recognize or encourage attempts at this record. It was deemed hazardous to health.

What Do You Mean, "Play Money"?

In the fall and winter of 1973, newspapers and magazines began carrying advertisements for the Monopoly Sweepstakes. No purchase was required. The entrant had only to list his or her name, address, zip code, and the name of his or her favorite toy store. At a random drawing conducted on January 24, 1974, a winning card was selected from the 701,115 entries, and Susan Bell of Paris, Tennessee, became the sweepstakes winner. Her prize? A Monopoly set, filled with $15,000 in real money. U.S. currency, that is.

Most Monopoly sets come equipped with the private currency printed by Parker Brothers, and the prosperity of their mint could end the woes of the World Bank. Since 1935, when they first began publishing the game, Parker Brothers have printed—or minted, if you wish—one trillion two hundred and sixteen billion Monopoly dollars. If you like zeroes, that's $1,216,-000,000,000. But that, admittedly, is a composite figure. Let's look just at one year: 1974.

Monopoly's mint produced $56,392,000,000.

The U.S. mint produced $2,897,080,000.

In an effort to combine both currencies to the benefit of our buying power, an exhibition game was held in November of 1973. The players were Brian Nuttall, the champion of Great Britain (and an actual real estate broker); Lee Bayrd of Los Angeles, then American Western champion; Don Lifton of Detroit, an attorney and current champion of the USMA's Midwest Regional Men's Invitational Monopoly Tournament; and Russell Smith, chairman of the Manhattan Savings Bank, who was playing Monopoly for the first time in his life. Naturally, he was the Banker. They played a game of Monopoly using real money so, naturally, the game was held in Mr. Smith's bank. At one point, the Monopoly Bank ran out of money, so officials of the real bank had to have additional funds drawn out of the vault. The game stopped at the end of an hour and a half of play, with no clear winner. All funds were returned.

Once, however, a lack of funds proved a much more serious event. It happened during the 161–hour marathon game played at the University of Pittsburgh in 1961. After days of play, it became obvious that the Bank was about to be broken. The players grew desperate. Loath to draw up the scrip that is permissible in such cases, they sent a wire to Parker Brothers, explaining their predicament and urgently requesting one million dollars to ward off another depression. Parker responded with commendable flair. They quickly wrapped a million dollars of Monopoly money and sent it by plane to Pittsburgh. While the shipment was still airborne, they sent a wire to the Pittsburgh branch of Brink's. An armored car was dispatched to the airport to meet the plane, and the money was delivered to the destitute marathon Bank under armed guard.

Here, There, and Just About Everywhere

In 1935, the American public made a bestseller out of a new game called Monopoly. Since then, nearly eighty million sets have been sold in this country alone. Every year, more Monopoly games are sold than were sold the year before. In 1974, sales totaled three and one-half million. Sets.

The game, under Parker Brothers' franchise, is marketed in twenty-five countries, and has been translated into fifteen languages: French, Italian, Spanish, German, Dutch, Flemish, Swedish, Danish, Norwegian, Greek, Portuguese, Japanese, Chinese, Hebrew, and English (British). Different Spanish versions are used in Colombia, Spain, and Venezuela.

In most cases, the property locations take the name of foreign real estate, and the dollars are translated into the local currency.

Most of the boards and properties look quite similar, despite the language differences. Piccadilly is just as yellow as Marvin Gardens, and the Rue de la Paix is just as blue as Boardwalk. There are occasional odd, unexpected differences, though. The Japanese set, which uses the American property names translated into Japanese symbols, has substituted its own illustrations for the locomotive that adorns the Railroad property deeds, and

for the Electric Company's light bulb and the Water Works' faucet.

AMERICAN	BRITISH	GERMAN	FRENCH	SPANISH
Boardwalk	Mayfair	Schlossallee	Rue de la Paix	Paseo del Prado
Park Place	Park Lane	Parkstrasse	Avenue des Champs Elysées	Paseo de la Castellana
New York Avenue	Vine Street	Berliner-strasse	Place Pigalle	Calle de Serrano
Marvin Gardens	Piccadilly	Goethestrasse	Rue Lafayette	Plaza de España

And the Chance and Community Chest cards from the Japanese set prove conclusively that we see what we expect to see. The art work is reproduced from the American cards, but seen in the context of Japanese symbols, the little mustached rich man suddenly looks surprisingly Oriental.

The Russian government banned the game for being "too capitalistic," but the Russian people have evinced strong interest in Monopoly and have made it a part of their underground culture. Of course, since sets are not permitted into the country, the resourceful citizenry have had to resort to unorthodox methods of obtaining them. During the 1959 American National Exhibition in Moscow, there were six Monopoly sets on display. By the time the exhibit closed, all six sets had disappeared.

Now that it seems to have conquered Earth, Monopoly is going on to greater heights and depths. During the sixty-day submersion of the U.S. nuclear submarine *Seawolf,* Monopoly turned out to be one of the crew's most popular diversions. Not known as a classical Navy game, it's sudden nautical popularity was explained by one of the sub's officers. It seems the men thrived on the fierce competition the game provided.

When NASA sends four astronauts on a proposed three year trip to Mars, the men will be confined together in close quarters, with no wives around. Psychology professor Dr. William J. Beausay feels that the men will require various sports and games to provide amusement and stimulation. He proposes that the crew play not merely isolated games, but three-year-long tournaments, with cash prizes awarded by NASA to the winners when they return. His reason: "All men must have an awfully strong motivator to compensate for the loss of sex for three years." He intends to examine the personalities of Monopoly players to see if the game is suitable for space, and expects to recommend that a set be included in the spaceship's supplies.

At NASA's request, Parker Brothers has already constructed two special Monopoly sets made with non-combustible paper supplied by the space agency itself. The houses and hotels are made of aluminum. Although NASA has no plans at present to include Monopoly on a forthcoming space flight, there's nothing like being prepared.

What? That Old Game?

Despite the facts, figures, and incredible statistics, it's still difficult to know why this, of all games, keeps going on and on and on. Its popularity, far from being diminished, is now greater than ever. No other proprietary game (chess and checkers are not owned by anyone) has ever been so enduringly popular.

Professional game inventors and analysts have pet theories about the role of games in man's cultural and psychological life. One notion has it that game exist to soothe the psychic bruises inflicted by everyday life. They offer romance; the rules of the everyday world do not apply. When all the tokens line up at the starting square, everyone is equal. The only discriminator is the dice.

Marvin Glass, the late dean of game designers, claimed that "a game . . . is like role playing. It's a drama. It takes you out of the situation you're living in and puts you in a new one. A game applies, therefore, more to the libido than to the superego. It's a fantasy, not a teaching machine."

And Aldous Huxley, speaking of board games in general, offered a theory on their timeless appeal: "With their simple and unequivocal rules, [games] are like so many islands of order in the vague untidy chaos of experience. In games one passes from the incomprehensible universe of given

reality into a neat little man-made world where everything is clear, purposive and easy to understand."

Maybe. Or maybe the factors are slightly less esthetic. Edward P. Parker, president of Parker Brothers from 1968 to 1973, said that "people like to clobber their best friends without actually doing any damage. That's the basis for practically every successful game."

Parker, who certainly should have known, analyzed what types of games appeal to people. "People want choices in their games. They want to think that if they make the right choices they can win the damn thing. There's still got to be an element of chance, of course, so the family dunce can turn out to be a genius every once in a while. But skill—making the right judgments— has got to enter into it, too."

In this, Parker seems to concur quite closely with the theory of Dr. Joyce Brothers, who claims that "the skill and luck factors in Monopoly are reassuring to many people. There is enough skill so if you win you can compliment yourself on being the best player, and enough luck so if you lose you can blame it on the dice. It can be very comforting."

Even *Life* magazine got into the game-analyzing business awhile back, and came up with some similar conclusions. "The last great non-word game was Monopoly, an inspired invention of the '30's that was perfectly attuned to the times. It so intensified a player's cupidity that it turned mother against son, brother against brother, as they tried to corner Atlantic City real estate."

But Shelly Berman summed it up. He claims that the joy of Monopoly comes from the premium placed on bad sportsmanship. "It's that thrill you get when you know you've wiped out a friend."

You needn't bring malice with you to the board, but a strong desire to win can't hurt. Even if you're just playing as a diversion, don't be surprised to find yourself becoming increasingly gleeful whenever an opponent lands on your property.

Happy playing.

2
Understanding the Rules

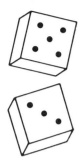

It may seem elementary, but many people play Monopoly with only a vague knowledge of the precise rules. There is great danger here: some of the fine print contains rules that are of great advantage to the player who knows them, and of potential harm to one who does not.

For instance, suppose you're playing a game with three other players. The player on your left lands on Oriental Avenue (with no houses); you own it. He glances at the Bank, to see if the property is for sale. The Title Deed is not in the Bank, so he knows that somebody owns Oriental Avenue. He says nothing.

You are busy arranging your money or something, and you haven't even noticed where your opponent has landed. You say nothing.

The player opposite you picks up the dice—it's now his turn. He tosses them, and you look up to see what's happening. At this point, you notice the token sitting on Oriental Avenue.

"Hey," you say, startled, "that's mine. I own Oriental."

"Too late," says the player who had landed there. "The next player has already thrown the dice."

"That doesn't matter," you protest. "You landed on my property. You owe me $6, please."

"Sorry," he grins cunningly. "You didn't ask early enough. Once the next player has thrown the dice, you lose your chance to collect the rent. Look it up in the rules if you don't believe me."

So you do, and you find to your dismay that he's right.

Your opponent in this case has done nothing illegal. He has simply made himself familiar with the fine points of all the rules of Monopoly. The rules are essentially simple, but there are some subtle nuances and technicalities that are easily overlooked. There are also some points of common confusion which can lead to major disagreements. Arguments over differing interpretations have strained bonds of friendship, chilled the bloom of budding romance, and occasionally led to lifelong feuds. As a safety precaution, then, as well as ammunition to improve your winning chances, learn the precise rules of Monopoly before you embark further on your playing career.

A copy of the rules, as they appear in each Monopoly set, is printed at the end of this book. This section examines and explains in detail some of the fine points and clarifies some of the obscurities and ambiguities.*

The Object of the Game

The object of Monopoly is to become the richest player on the board, in terms of total assets—cash, property, and buildings—and to drive all of your opponents into bankruptcy. You accomplish this by buying, selling, renting, and trading properties in the most profitable way.

The Players

Two to eight people can play Monopoly. Naturally, the strategies involved in playing only one or two opponents will be very different from those used in playing against six or seven other players. The smaller the game, the greater the chances that players will acquire complete color groups near the beginning of the game, and the more chance you have of simply landing—by luck—on all three properties of a color group. The larger the game, the more difficult it will be for any player to acquire all the properties of a group, and the less chance each of you will have to obtain that property group simply by lucky throws of the dice. Property trading among players is a necessary skill in games of any size, but it is obviously more complex and devious when many players are involved.

---

* There are many variations to the basic game of Monopoly. Some of the more common variations are discussed at the end of this section. But the main purpose here, indeed, the object of this book, is concerned with the strategies of how to win at the basic, official, and intriguing game of Monopoly.

Preparing the Cards

This is not in the rules, but as you're setting up the board to play a game of Monopoly, be sure you shuffle each deck of cards thoroughly: the pack of Community Chest cards and the pack of Chance cards. Do this even if the set is new. The cards come from the factory in an established order; shuffling them produces a more random distribution.

The Bank keeps the pack of Title Deeds and should display them so that the players can see which properties are still for sale. Place the shuffled packs of yellow Community Chest cards and the orange Chance cards face down on the board in the appropriate spaces.

The Banker

The Banker must be honest, efficient, and good at arithmetic. Perhaps most importantly, he must have a good sense of humor. His duties will include paying each player the proper salary each time that player's token passes or lands on GO (moving in a forward direction), selling property and buildings, holding mortgages, buying back buildings, and auctioning property. He should be familiar with all rules governing his activities.

If more than one player wishes to be the Banker, throw the dice to determine who it should be. And if no one wants the job, each player should throw the dice. The person throwing either the highest or the lowest number gets the job, according to the decision you've made beforehand.

The Banker must keep his money separate from the Bank's at all times.

The Bank

The Bank is a venerable institution. Backed by Parker Brothers rather than the F.D.I.C., this cornucopia is the source of all Monopoly wealth: real estate, cash, and buildings. The Bank dispenses salaries (the $200 you get each time you pass GO); bonuses ("Bank pays you dividend of $50"); prizes ("You have won Second Prize in a Beauty Contest . . ."); and other unexpected windfalls dictated by Chance and the Community Chest.

It also collects money from all sales and penalties. When a player lands on a property he wants, he may buy it from the Bank. When he builds a house on that property, he buys the building from the Bank. And when he's then assessed for street repairs ("$40 per house; $115 per hotel"), he leaves his money, and his tears, at the friendly neighborhood Bank.

But this Bank has some special functions: it acts as Auctioneer whenever a player lands on an unowned property and decides not to buy it. The property is then offered by the Banker to the highest bidder. Bidding may start at any price, and the original player (the one who declined to buy the property when he landed on it) has the option of bidding on the property, along with everyone else.

(Unlike banks in the real world, *the Monopoly Bank can never go broke!* If you play a very long game, or a game with many people, the Bank may run out of cash. However, being the sole monetary institution of the State of Monopoly, the Bank has the authority to issue as much additional money as may be needed to continue the game. If your Monopoly Bank becomes short of funds, simply use slips of paper to mint some additional cash.)

Buildings

Each Monopoly set comes equipped with twelve hotels and thirty-two houses. This number is deliberate. There are not enough buildings to place on all the available building lots, so it's a matter of first come, first served. If the Bank runs out of buildings, you may *not* add more houses or hotels to the set. Any player who wants to construct more buildings on his property must wait until someone else sells buildings back to the Bank.

Chance and Community Chest

Place the shuffled packs of yellow Community Chest cards, and the orange

Chance cards, *face down* on the board. Each time a player lands on a Chance or a Community Chest square, he takes the top card from the appropriate deck, reads the instructions, and obeys them. By custom, the card is often shown to the opponents, but this is not a rule.

After you've followed the instructions on the card, return it *face down* to the bottom of the deck.

Get Out of Jail, Free . . . Both the Chance and the Community Chest decks contain a Get Out of Jail, Free card. If you draw one of these, don't put it back. Just hold it until you land in Jail: the card can then be used to get you out. If you don't want the card, you can sell it to another player, at any time, at a price you both agree on. You cannot sell the card to the Bank. (Why should the Bank worry about getting out of Jail?) If and when the Get Out of Jail, Free card is used, it should be returned to the bottom of the deck, face down.

NOTE: Although the Get Out of Jail, Free card has no intrinsic monetary value, if you use it to get yourself out from behind bars, it provides you a savings of $50. Thus, if you have the card, you might offer it to your opponent for somewhat less than $50 (or more if he's not thinking too clearly). Obviously, if an opponent offers the card to you, you should pay less than $50 for it. If your opponent holds out for $50 or more, forget it. Why pay $70 for the card, when it would only cost you $50 to pay the bailiff directly to bail yourself out of Jail?

NOTE: In totaling up your assets, the Get Out of Jail, Free card has absolutely *no* monetary worth. (See further discussions of this card below.)

Chance and Community Chest Confusions

Herein lie some of the misunderstandings and ambiguities that lead to the discussions that often make Monopoly so lively.

Ouch! These are painful cards to draw, especially far into the game, when you've been doing a lot of building. But don't make them more painful than they're intended to be.

First of all, remember that you pay on the basis of the buildings *you*

own, regardless of how many buildings your opponent owns. Ignore his; count up only your own houses and hotels.

Next, remember that your payment is based on the number of buildings you have standing on the board. It's true that before you bought your red hotel, you had four green houses standing on that same building lot. But those houses aren't there anymore, so don't be foolish enough to pay for their memory. What's on the piece of property *right now?* One hotel? O.K., then all you pay for is the repair cost for one hotel.

Now, what if you *used to* have two houses on Oriental Avenue, but you had to sell them to get some cash. Do you own the houses any more? No. So should you pay a repair cost for houses you used to own? Of course not.

Here are some examples of how to figure out your repair costs:

If you draw one of these cards, and do not own any houses or hotels *at this moment* (that is, at the time you draw the card, there are no houses or hotels standing on any of your property), you're in luck. Flash the card so your opponent can see it, turn the card face down, and put it underneath its pack. Smile.

If you draw one of these cards and you own only hotels, these hotels are all you pay for. For example, let's suppose you own three hotels, and you draw the Chance card. It will cost you $100 to repair each of the hotels: $3 \times \$100 = \$300$. Grit your teeth, and pay the Bank $300.

If you draw one of these cards and you own several houses and hotels, add up the numbers of houses *you* own, multiply by the cost for repairs per house, do the same for your hotels, and hope you've got enough money to pay for it all. For example, suppose you own five houses and two hotels, and you draw the Community Chest card. You are assessed $40 for each house. $5 \times \$40 = \$200$. You are also assessed $115 per hotel. $2 \times \$115 = \$230$. You must pay the bank a total of $430.

What do you mean you don't have it? Then get it. Will you have to mortgage some of your property to raise the cash? Fine, but remember that you cannot mortgage a piece of property if there is even one building standing on any property of that color group.

Example: **Marvin Gardens** **Ventnor Avenue** **Atlantic Avenue**

Suppose you own the Yellow properties and have a house standing on Ventnor Avenue. You need to borrow some money from the Bank, so you decide to mortgage Marvin Gardens. Uh, uh, sorry. Before you can mortgage any of these three building lots, you'll have to get rid of the house first. Since houses cannot be mortgaged, this means you must *sell* the house back to the Bank at one-half its cost. Houses on the Yellow group cost $150 apiece, so you can return your house to the Bank for $75. And now, if you wish, you can mortgage Marvin Gardens—or any of the others of this group.

Now, here's an interesting problem. You *had* five houses and two hotels when you drew the Community Chest card, right? But you've just sold one of the houses in order to raise the money to pay the Street Repairs bill. Now you have only four houses. Are you only assessed for these four?

No. You must pay the Bank for the number of houses or hotels you owned *at the time you landed on Community Chest*. Even if you had to sell

Chance Advance token to the nearest Railroad and pay owner Twice the Rental to which he is otherwise entitled.
If Railroad is unowned, you may buy it from the Bank.

all of your buildings to raise the money to pay the bill, you must still compute the amount due on the basis of the number of houses and hotels you owned at the time you drew the card.

Which Railroad is the nearest, if your token is in between two? The Railroad that is *in front* of you. There is a Chance card that specifically instructs you to move backwards ("Go back 3 spaces"), but, with this one exception, *always* move your token *forward* (clockwise) as you move around the board (in the direction indicated by the GO arrow).

Look at this section of the Monopoly board. Suppose you landed on the Chance square that is in between the Short Line Railroad and Park Place. Even though there is a Railroad just behind your token, when the card tells you to move to the nearest Railroad, you must move your token *forward*, around GO, to the Reading Railroad. Then obey the rest of the directions on the card.

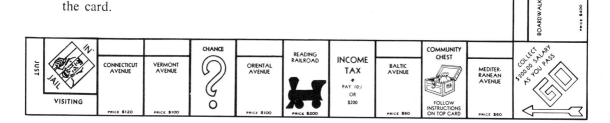

Incidentally, since your token passed GO in this case, you would collect $200 while en route to the Reading.

The card says that if the Railroad is owned, ". . . pay owner twice the rental to which he is otherwise entitled." If he owns only the Railroad on which you've landed, the *normal* rent would be $25; since you must pay him twice that, you must pay $50. If he owns two other Railroads, for a total of three, the *normal* rent for landing on any one of the three would be $100. So you would have to pay $200.

Suppose you're lucky and no one owns the Railroad. Read the rest of the card: "If the Railroad is unowned, you may buy it from the Bank." You may, 43 but you don't have to if you don't want to. If you decide not to buy the unowned Railroad, simply refuse the offer—but if you do, the Bank then puts the Railroad up for auction. Any player, including yourself, may now bid to purchase the Railroad.

The trip to the Reading is profitable, and the ride sounds nice, but what happens when you finally put your token down on the Reading Railroad? Very simple: the same thing that would have happened if you had landed on the Reading normally. If your opponent owns it, and it's not mortgaged, pay him the normal rent, depending upon how many other Railroads he owns (regardless of whether they're mortgaged or not). If no one owns the Reading, you may buy it yourself. If you don't want it, the Bank will put it up for auction. And even though the card doesn't specifically mention it, if your token passes GO, collect $200 on your way to Illinois. If the property is unowned, you may use this $200 to buy it—if you want it.

The whole secret to interpreting this card correctly is simply to do precisely what it says. First, move your token *forward* to the nearest Utility (Electric Company or Water Works). If you pass GO, collect $200.

Normally, if you land on a Utility which is owned by your opponent, you immediately look up to see whether he owns one or both of them. If he owns only the one you landed on, multiply the dice total by four, and pay him that amount. If he owns both Utilities, you pay him ten times the amount thrown on your dice.

If you are ordered to move your token to a Utility by a Chance card, however, the procedure is different. In this case, it doesn't matter how many Utilities your opponent owns. If he owns the one you landed on, simply do as the card says: toss the dice again. Let's say you now get a and a which equals seven. The card says "pay owner a total ten times the amount thrown. So $10 \times 7 = 70$, and you pay your rotten opponent $70.

If no one owns the Utility, of course, you may buy it, if you want it. And if you don't, the Bank will put it up for auction. If you draw a card

that advances your token to a building lot which is owned, you must pay the appropriate rent to your opponent. If, for instance, you land on St. Charles Place and there are no houses on it, you would only have to pay the owner the base rate of $10. If your opponent has the other two Maroon title deeds—Virginia and States Avenues—you would pay $20 for landing on St. Charles. (The normal rent is doubled if the owner has the complete color group.) And if, unhappily (for you), St. Charles Place happens to have three houses on it, you would have to pay the owner $450, the price for renting St. Charles with three houses.

If you're lucky enough to land on a building lot that no one owns, you

45

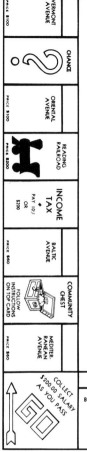

may buy it from the Bank if you would like it. If you choose not to buy it, however, remember that the Bank will put it up for auction.

When a card directs you to place your token directly on GO, you collect $200 the moment you reach the GO square. You do *not* receive an additional $200 on your next turn, when your token moves past GO. You've already collected your salary for this turn.

Suppose, however, that your token is on Luxury Tax; you pick up the dice and you roll a four (landing your token on Community Chest) or a nine (landing your token on Chance). You turn over the card, and it tells you to "Advance to GO—Collect $200." Do you collect $200 or $400?

Let's take it step by step. First, you tossed the dice and moved your token around GO. That earned you $200. Next, you landed on Chance or Community Chest, and the card told you to move your token to GO. You can't move backwards, so the card obviously means that you should move your token forward around the board again. When you finally reach GO, you're thus at the start of a new turn, which qualifies you to collect another $200 salary. In this particular example, then, you would collect a total of $400. Nice bit of luck.

46

This one is normally clear enough. A question does arise, however, in a situation like the one described above. You roll the dice, move your token past GO, then land on either Chance or Community Chest and draw a Go to Jail card. Do you collect the $200 for going past GO? Yes, you do. You passed GO *before* you drew the card, so you earned your $200 salary legally. This can only happen if your token starts out on the fourth (last) side of the board, where the Greens and Dark Blues are. Your token then has to pass GO on its way to the Chance or Community Chest square. As long as your token starts out on any other side of the board, follow the normal rules stated on the card: go directly to Jail, do not pass GO, and do not collect $200.

Buying and Trading Property

Buying Property from the Bank

According to the official rules, "Whenever a player lands on an unowned property he may buy that property from the Bank at its printed price. He receives the Title Deed card showing ownership and places it face-up in front of him."

"Whenever" means just that: whenever. If you roll the dice, move your token the designated number of spaces, and find yourself on an unowned piece of property, you may buy it if you wish. If you draw a Chance or Community Chest card which instructs you to move your token to a certain place, and that place turns out to be an unowned piece of property, you may buy it—if you wish.

If you decline the offer in either case, and refuse to buy the piece of property, *the Bank immediately puts it up for auction.*

Buying Property at Auction

The Banker acts as Auctioneer, and starts the bidding by offering the property to all players—including you—even if you're the one who just landed on the property and refused to buy it. (This gives you a chance to change your mind, once you find out what your opponent is trying to do.)

Bidding may start at any amount. Theoretically, a piece of property could be sold for one dollar, though this is rather unlikely. (But it certainly has happened!) The player to offer the highest bid wins the right to buy the property. He must then pay the Bank the full amount that he has bid, and the Title Deed is his.

Buying When You're Short on Cash

If you want to buy a piece of tempting property from the Bank, but you don't have enough cash to cover the cost, you do have several options. Just remember, though, that whatever you do to raise the money, ultimately you must be able to pay the Bank the full purchase price. You cannot buy real estate "on time."

It is perfectly legal to sell any buildings you own (at one-half their purchase price) or mortgage another piece of property in order to raise the cash you need. It is *not* legal, however, to mortgage the property you are in the midst of buying.

In other words, suppose you land on Ventnor Avenue and want to buy it, but you don't have the necessary $260. You hand the Bank $130 in cash and propose to pay the balance in the following novel way: first, the Bank is to give you the Title Deed for Ventnor. You will then turn it face down in front of you, declare it mortgaged, receive the $130 mortgage money from the Bank, and hand this same $130 back to the Bank in payment for the ownership of the now-mortgaged Ventnor. Ingenious, but illegal. No property can be mortgaged until *after* it has been fully paid for.

Trading: Buying Property from Another Player

Essentially, there are no rules governing private enterprise between players, as long as the Bank is not involved in the purchase or sale of the piece of property, and as long as no buildings are involved. Houses and hotels may *not* be sold or traded by one player to another. This is purely a Bank function. If one or more buildings are standing on the property you want to sell or trade, or on any other property of that color group, all of the buildings must be sold back to the Bank before you can get rid of the property.

Trading discussions and negotiations may occur at any time, but the actual trade may only be consummated during your or your trading partner's turn, or *between* the turns of other players. In practice, most players make it a house rule to permit the actual trade to take place only during the turn of one of the other traders. Before you begin your game, decide which method you want to use, and be certain all players understand and agree to it.

Any property trade or sale between players is legal as long as it is mutually agreeable to them. You may sell one or more undeveloped properties (with no buildings standing on them or on any other building lot of that color group) to an opponent in return for money or other properties, or a combination of both. You may also make some other personal arrangement if your opponent agrees to it. You may, for instance, give your opponent Pacific Avenue in return for Oriental, as perhaps the trade will give both of you complete color groups. But your opponent will be gaining the high-priced Greens, while you would acquire the low-priced Light Blue group, so you might demand another concession in your trade.

There are many house rules stipulating what is and what is not permissible, and trading agreements often become quite complex. To minimize bloodshed, such agreements must be made before the sale or trade is completed, and must then be considered binding.

Trading to Avoid Bankruptcy

If you are faced with a debt you cannot pay, and are thus about to go bankrupt, you may attempt to make a trade either with your creditor (if it is 49 another player and not the Bank), or with another player. There is a restriction, however. If you owe money to Player Two, you may only trade or sell your property to Player Three if you will gain enough cash to pay the debt in full. You cannot deliberately cheat your creditor by selling your property for a small amount of money. You cannot trade valuable properties for Player Three's less valuable properties either, as this, too, would obviously be a deliberate attempt to cheat your creditor. (For a fuller discussion of this situation, see Bankruptcy, page 75.)

Buying Buildings

When a player owns all of the properties in a color group he may purchase buildings from the Bank (if the Bank has buildings available), erect them on these properties, and begin the real road to riches.

The rules state that you may build houses or hotels at any time, but this has to be somewhat qualified.

a) You may buy and erect buildings at any time during your turn. From the time the preceding player completes moving his token and acting on the result of that move (obeying the Chance or Community Chest card, or paying rent if he has landed on someone else's property, etc.), and the dice pass into your possession, it is considered your turn. It remains your turn until you, too, have completed throwing the dice, moving your token and acting on the result of that move. (If you throw doubles, naturally your turn ends upon the completion of the final play.) At any time during this period, you may interrupt the course of your turn to purchase one or more buildings on your vacant lots.

b) You may buy and erect buildings at any time *between* the turns of other players. Suppose you're playing a game with three other people. We'll consider you Player One. Your opponents are Players Two, Three, and Four. You complete your turn, and Player Two picks up the dice. He shakes. He tosses. The dice land. It's a seven. In seven moves, his token will land on Marvin Gardens, which you own.

Marvin Gardens has only one house on it at the moment, and somehow you've come into a bit of ready cash. You eye the board eagerly, mentally counting the squares. If you mortgage the Water Works, you can just afford three more houses on Marvin. . . . That would nearly wipe out Player Two.

Uh, uh. Sorry. That's called taking advantage. It's also called unfair.

Player Two is still in the middle of his turn. He has already tossed the dice, and until he moves his token to Marvin Gardens and pays you the rent due for the one house that was there at the time of his throw, it is still his turn. You cannot erect additional houses on Marvin Gardens or anywhere else until Player Two completes his turn and the dice pass to Player Three. You may then tell Player Three to wait, while you put up your new buildings.

NOTE: Many players find it easier to build *only on their own turns*. This house rule is so common that in many places it is the norm. Before beginning your game, discuss this point with your opponents and decide which rule you wish to follow.

Building Must Be Done Evenly

Suppose you own the Maroon properties: Virginia Avenue, States Avenue, and St. Charles Place. Houses on each of these building lots cost $100 apiece, and you have earmarked $200 of your savings for buying houses. The Bank sells you two houses.

Q: Where can you put them?

A: You may put the first house on any of these building lots, and the second house on another of the lots. You may *not* put both houses on the same piece of property. That would give you two houses on one lot while the other two lots in your color group stand empty.

Let's suppose that you set your first houses up like this:

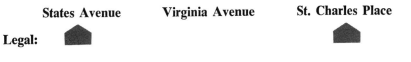

A few turns later, you have some more money to invest: $300 this time. You buy three more houses from the Bank, to be placed on this same group.

The first of these houses *must* be placed on Virginia Avenue, to even out the properties.

Q: What if you want to put all three of the new houses on Virginia Avenue? Can you?

A: No. That would give you three houses on Virginia, and only one house on each of the other two properties, like this:

In this case, you own three properties, and a total of five houses. You must place two houses on two of the properties, and one house on the remaining property, like this:

If at some time in the future you buy one more house, you would have no choice as to where it should go. The next house would have to be erected on St. Charles Place, to keep the property development even. It's an interesting, if controversial, theory of urban development. The rule for building evenly extends only to the properties of one color group. If you own more than one color group (lucky you), you do not have to build evenly across both of them. It is perfectly legal not to put any buildings on one color group, and spend all your money erecting houses or hotels on the other. If necessary, you may even mortgage some of the properties of the first group in order to raise the cash to buy houses for the other one. Determining which group to develop when is one of the major strategies of the game.

Buying Hotels

52 Hotels may be built according to most of the same regulations as those stated

above for houses. You may purchase your first hotel only after you have constructed four houses on *every* property of a color group. If you have built four houses on States Avenue and four houses on Virginia, but only three houses on St. Charles Place, you must buy another house on St. Charles Place before you can construct a hotel on any of these properties.

States Avenue   **Virginia Avenue**   **St. Charles Place**

Legal:

Q: Can you build a hotel on Virginia right now?

A: No. First you must buy a fourth house for St. Charles Place; then you can buy your hotel on Virginia Avenue.

Again, it's the principle of building evenly. Now, suppose you really want to see that hotel rise over the heights of Virginia, and you can't bear to wait another turn. If you have enough money, there's no problem. Buy the house for St. Charles and the hotel for Virginia during the same turn. That's perfectly legal. (If you're playing with a stickler for the rules, just plunk down your money for the house, put the house *in position* on St. Charles Place, and then negotiate your hotel transaction. It's all a matter of proper sequence.)

Q: Can you build hotels immediately, without constructing houses first?

A: If you've got your own private bank, you might be able to swing it. Remember the cardinal rule, though: all building must be done evenly.

The rules state that you can't buy a hotel until every property in a color group has four houses standing on it. If you're rich enough to go in for some major building construction, and if the Bank has enough buildings for sale, you could manage to acquire a hotel all at once, in one of two ways:

a) you could plunk down enough cash to buy four houses all at once, on each of the building lots of this color group, plus the cost of five houses on the lot you want your hotel on (a hotel costs the equivalent of five   53 houses, which is the same as paying the Bank for one more house, and then turning in the four houses you purchased previously). In this way, you'd wind up with something like this:

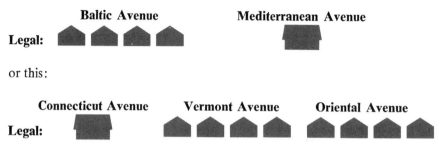

or this:

or

b) if you've got even more money stashed away, you could buy two or more of your hotels simultaneously:

Remember, though, that in a three-lot group, if you want to build two hotels at the same time (for the cost of five houses each), you must still construct a minimum of four houses on the remaining lot.

You may not construct any hotels until each building lot of this group has four houses on it.

Of course, in the even more unlikely possibility that you have enough money to construct three hotels simultaneously, you can simply pay the Bank the cost of five houses for each of the three properties—that is, the cost of fifteen houses—and plunk down your three red hotels, all in a row, much to the chagrin of your opponents. Instant metropolis!

NOTE: If the Bank has a building shortage, you have a problem. You *cannot* buy a hotel unless the Bank has enough houses for you to construct four on each lot of your color group—including the lot you want the hotel on. Remember: technically, you buy a hotel by paying the Bank the cost of the fifth house plus the four houses already on that building lot.

Even if you have enough cash to purchase three hotels immediately (for a three-property group) the Bank must still have *available for sale* at least twelve houses.

If it has fewer houses, all you can do is buy them up, put them on your properties, and wait until someone else sells more houses back to the Bank.

Building Shortage

The rules say that when the Bank has no houses to sell, players wishing to build must wait for some player to turn back or to sell his houses to the Bank before building. If there are a limited number of houses and hotels available, and two or more players wish to buy more than the Bank has, the houses or hotels must be sold at auction to the highest bidder.

If you want to buy a house, and the Bank has no houses to sell, obviously there's nothing you can do but wait. *You cannot move a building from one of your lots to another.*

If you want to buy a hotel, first remember the build evenly rule. You must have at least four houses on every lot of a color group before you can construct a hotel on one of those lots. Suppose you have a great deal of money and want to build a hotel on Illinois Avenue. At the moment, you own one house on each of the Red building lots.

Kentucky	**Indiana**	**Illinois**

You are certainly willing and able to purchase three more houses for each lot (for a total of nine more houses), but the Bank only has four houses available. If you buy all four, and distribute them evenly, you will wind up with:

Kentucky **Indiana** **Illinois**

You may have enough money to purchase the rest of the houses, but since they're not available, this is the best that you can do. To do additional building, you must wait for someone to sell some houses back to the Bank.

But wait, you say. You have enough money to purchase hotels simultaneously on each of the three properties!

That's nice. Unfortunately, it doesn't help very much right now. It's true that a hotel costs the equivalent of five houses, but paying this sum is not enough. The houses themselves must be physically present. To build your hotel on Illinois, you must first have four houses on each of the three lots: a total of twelve houses. Only then can you turn back the four houses from Illinois, together with an additional $150 (the cost of a "fifth" house), and convert to your hotel.

NOTE: If the Bank has plenty of houses available, you can buy your three hotels simultaneously by paying the Bank the cost of fifteen houses— five for each lot. But this shortcut is only permissible because the houses are *there*. If your opponent gets technical, you can always do it the long way: purchase four houses for each property, then convert them into three hotels, all during the same turn.

If the Bank has one house available and both you and your opponent want to buy it, the Bank puts the building up for auction, and sells it to the highest bidder. Bidding starts at the lowest purchase price, determined by the properties on which you and your opponent want to erect the house. In other words, if you want to put the house on Connecticut, where houses cost $50 each, and your opponent wants to put the house on Tennessee, where each house costs $100, bidding will start at $50. There is no ceiling.

If there are a limited number of houses and/or hotels available, and two or more players are fighting to gain their ownership, the Bank may put all the contested buildings up for auction.

A building shortage can affect selling as well as buying. If you own three hotels on one color group, and need just a little cash, you may want to sell the equivalent of one house back to the Bank. Thus, you would retain two of the hotels, and convert the third hotel into four houses.

But if the Bank doesn't have four houses, you would have to sell *all* of your hotels back to the Bank for one-half their purchase cost.

Rent

When you land on a piece of property owned by your opponent, you must pay rent for the privilege of resting your token on that square. If the property is mortgaged, no rent can be collected for it. (When a property is mortgaged, its Title Deed card should be turned *face down* in front of the owner. The Title Deeds for all unmortgaged properties should be kept face-up, visible to all of the players at all times.)

When a property is mortgaged to the Bank, it still belongs to the mortgagee (the owner), not to the Bank. The Bank is simply holding it as collateral on the mortgage money it has loaned to the owner. Therefore, if you land on a mortgaged property, you do not pay rent to the owner, nor to the Bank. All rents are suspended until the mortgage is lifted.

You must pay rent *whenever* your token lands on an unmortgaged property, whether you got there by a throw of the dice or by instructions from a Chance or Community Chest card.

Remember the example given earlier. If you're the landlord, be sure to watch where your opponent moves. If he lands on your property, it's *your* responsibility to point this out to him and ask for your rent. If you don't notice that someone has landed on your property, and the next player picks up and tosses the dice, you've lost your opportunity. Legally, the player who landed on your property no longer has to pay the rent. You must ask for your rent *before* the next player throws the dice.

If you can't pay your rent: Normally, if you can't raise enough cash by selling, mortgaging or trading your holdings, you must declare bankruptcy. If your game permits house rules, and all players have agreed to this before play began, you may attempt to make some arrangement with your debtor.

The amount of rent you must pay for landing on any property changes according to several factors:

Paying Rent for Building Lots

a) If your opponent owns one or two building lots of a color group, but does not hold the complete color group, you pay only the base rent (the first, and lowest, rent listed on the Title Deed) if you land on that property.

b) Suppose your opponent owns all of the Title Deeds for one color group (all three Yellows, or all three Reds, etc.) and has no houses or hotels on any of the properties. If you land on one of them, the rent you pay is *double* the base rent (twice as much as the first, and lowest, rent listed on the Title Deed card). In other words, the owner of a property group can charge double rent for vacant lots in that group.

c) If your opponent owns a color group and has one or more houses on some of the properties in that group, but *no* houses or hotels on the property you land on, rent is double the base rent. Ignore the buildings on the other properties. Just remember that he owns the complete group, so the double-rent rule applies.

d) If your opponent owns a complete color group, and one or more of the properties in this group are mortgaged, but the property you land on is *not* mortgaged, you pay him double rent. Even though some of the properties are mortgaged, technically your opponent still owns the complete property group.

For example, suppose your opponent owns the Light Blues, but has mortgaged some of these properties: Oriental Avenue, mortgaged; Vermont Avenue, unmortgaged; Connecticut Avenue, mortgaged. And suppose, as luck would have it, that you land on Vermont Avenue, which has a base rent of $6. You would owe your opponent $12 rent.

e) If you land on a property which has one or more houses or a hotel on it, pay the rent according to the price list on the Title Deed.

f) If your opponent draws a Chance card which directs him to advance his token to your building lot ("Advance to Illinois Avenue"; "Advance token to Boardwalk"; "Advance to St. Charles Place") and you own the piece of property, your opponent must pay you the appropriate rent, just as he would if he had landed there normally.

Paying Rent for Utilities

a) Suppose you own only one Utility—either Water Works or Electric Company—and your opponent lands on it. Don't touch the dice! Take the total they show right now—the number which told your opponent how many spaces to move—and multiply that number by four. For example, suppose your opponent throws an eight, and moves his token to the Electric Company, which you own. To compute how much rent he owes you, consider his original throw of a [die] and a [die] for a total of eight. $8 \times 4 = \$32$ rent.

b) If you own both Utilities, the rent is ten times the amount shown on the dice. Suppose your opponent lands on either the Electric Company or Water Works. His dice show a [die] and a [die] for a total of nine. $9 \times 10 = \$90$ rent.

c) Suppose your opponent lands on Chance and draws the card telling him to advance his card to the nearest Utility.

If you own the Utility, your opponent must toss the dice *again*, and pay you ten times the amount shown on this new toss of the dice, whether you own one Utility or both!

Chance

ADVANCE TOKEN TO NEAREST UTILITY.

IF UNOWNED you may buy it from bank.

IF OWNED, throw dice and pay owner a total ten times the amount thrown.

© 1961 PARKER BROTHERS, INC.

d) Suppose you own both Utilities, but you have mortgaged the Electric Company. If your opponent lands on the Electric Company, he pays no rent to anyone. If he lands on Water Works, however, he must pay you *ten* times the amount shown on the dice, because you still own both Utilities. For purposes of computing the rent, it does not matter that the other Utility is mortgaged.

Paying Rent for Railroads

The rent for a single Railroad is $25. But unlike the color card groups, which double in value only when all of the Title Deeds in a group are owned, transportation charges for each Railroad increase with each additional Railroad you own.

If you own one RR the rent to your passengers is $25.

If you own two RRs the rent to your passengers is $50.

If you own three RRs the rent to your passengers is $100.

If you own all four RRs the rent to your passengers is $200.

a) Suppose you own the Reading Railroad and the Short Line Railroad, and your opponent lands on the Short Line. He must pay you $50.

b) Suppose you own the Pennsylvania Railroad and the B&O Railroad, but the Pennsylvania Railroad is mortgaged. If your opponent lands on the Pennsylvania, he pays no rent to anyone. If he lands on the B&O, he must pay you $50. When figuring out how much rent is due, forget about the fact that the other Railroad is mortgaged. Just remember that you own *two* Railroads, so your opponent must pay the rate for two.

c) Suppose your opponent lands on Chance and draws the card telling him to "take a ride on the Reading. If you pass GO collect $200." All right. If he passes GO, your opponent will collect his $200 salary from the Bank. But how much rent does he pay you if you own the Reading Railroad?

It depends on how many other Railroads you own. Look at the rent on the chart above (or the chart printed on each of the Railroad Title Deeds) and charge your opponent accordingly. Remember, it doesn't matter whether or not you have mortgaged some of the other Railroads. They still belong to you.

d) Suppose your opponent draws the Chance card that tells him to "advance token to the nearest Railroad and pay owner twice the rental to which he is otherwise entitled." If you own three Railroads: the B&O, the Reading, and the Short Line, the normal rent for landing on any of the three would be $100. If your opponent advances his token to the B&O, he must obey the instructions on the Chance card and pay you twice this amount: $200.

Mortgaging

The only way to borrow money is to take out a Bank loan by mortgaging a piece of your property. This can be done at any time throughout the game; you need not wait for your turn. You may not borrow money from (or lend money to) another player. You may not mortgage any property if there are one or more buildings on it, *or* if there are any buildings on any other properties of that color group. If you have a complete group with one or more buildings on any of the properties, you must sell *all* of the buildings—houses and hotels—back to the Bank before you can mortgage *any* of the properties in that color group.

New York Avenue   **Tennessee Avenue**   **St. James Place**

If you own the Orange properties, and want to mortgage Tennessee Avenue, you will first have to sell the house on Tennessee back to the Bank. But you will also have to sell the house on New York! You cannot mortgage Tennessee until there are *no* houses on any of these three properties.

Buildings are not mortgageable; they can only be *sold* back to the Bank for one-half their purchase price.   61

Mortgages are for one-half the purchase price of the piece of property. The mortgage value is printed on the back of each Title Deed card. When you mortgage a piece of property, turn over the Title Deed so that it is face down in front of you, with the mortgage side up.

You may not collect rent on a mortgaged property—either a building lot, a Railroad, or a Utility. But you *can* collect rent on any unmortgaged properties that you may own within the same real estate group. In other words, if you own both Indiana and Illinois Avenues, and you have had to mortgage Illinois, you can still collect rent if your opponent lands on Indiana Avenue.

If you have an unimproved color group—for instance, Indiana, Illinois, and Kentucky Avenues (the Red building lots)—with no houses on any of these properties, the rent for each property is, of course, *doubled*. ("If a player owns ALL the lots of any color group, the rent is doubled on unimproved lots in that group.") If you then have to mortgage any of these lots —for instance, Illinois Avenue—and your opponent lands on one of the unmortgaged properties—Kentucky, let's say—you may still charge him *double* rent for that property. You still retain ownership of the complete group, even though one or more of the title cards from that group are mortgaged.

NOTE: You may *not* mortgage a property for purposes of raising the money to buy it from the Bank. If you land on Oriental Avenue, which costs $100, you may *not* ask the Bank for the Title Deed, immediately turn the Title Deed over to its mortgaged side, ask the Bank for $50 for the mortgage, then combine the Bank's $50 with another $50 of your own, and use this money to purchase Oriental. You must raise the money some other way; a piece of property cannot be mortgaged until you have established complete ownership of it by paying the Bank the full purchase price.

If, however, you are buying Oriental from an *opponent,* and if he agrees to wait a moment for his money, you may use the Bank to help finance the transaction. Buy Oriental, immediately turn the Title Deed over to its mortgaged side and place it down in front of you. Then collect the $50 mortgage from the Bank and give it to your opponent as part of your payment for the property. You will then *own* Oriental, although it will be mortgaged until you raise enough cash to get it out of hock.

Lifting a Mortgage

To get a piece of property out of hock, you must repay the Bank the amount of money it has lent you (the amount of the mortgage), plus 10 percent interest for the Bank's services. This 10 percent is based on the amount of the mortgage, not on the original price of the property.

Suppose you have mortgaged New York Avenue. The property originally cost you $200 when you bought it, but the Bank will give you only half this amount—$100—as a mortgage. To lift this mortgage, you must pay the Bank the mortgage ($100) plus 10 percent of the mortgage (10 percent of $100). Thus, $110 will unmortgage New York Avenue.

If you have a complete color group, you may buy houses and hotels only when all of the properties of that group are no longer mortgaged. If you own New York, Tennessee, and St. James Place, and New York is still mortgaged, you may not buy a house on St. James Place. First you must unmortgage New York.

The mortgaged property is yours as long as you wish to retain it; no other player may obtain it against your wishes by repaying the Bank's mortgage and claiming the property as his own.

However, you may sell a mortgaged property to another player at any price you both agree on. The new owner has two options:

a) he may lift the mortgage at once by paying off the mortgage plus the original 10 percent interest to the Bank. If he doesn't want to unmortgage the property immediately, he may

b) immediately repay the original Bank interest of 10 percent, and then declare that he is not going to lift the mortgage right away. Later on, when he does want to unmortgage the piece of property, the new owner must repay the amount of the mortgage plus an *additional 10 percent* to the Bank.

You may also use a mortgaged property to pay a debt. If you owe the Bank any taxes, a fine, or the cost of building repairs, and you don't have enough cash, you can *give* the Bank a piece of mortgaged property in place of some or all of your debt. The property is worth the amount of the mortgage minus the 10 percent interest charge. If you give the Bank the mortgaged New York Avenue to cover your $125 tax bill, you still owe the Bank another $35.

	Mortgage Value − Interest = Cash Value		
New York	$100	− $10 =	$90

$125 tax bill
− 90 cash value
of New York Avenue
———
$ 35 balance due

When the Bank receives a piece of mortgaged property in this way, it immediately puts the property up for auction at the original (unmortgaged) price, and you or anyone else can bid for it.

If you owe money to your opponent, you can *offer* him a piece of mortgaged property to cover all or part of your debt. However, it is up to your opponent (your creditor) to decide:

a) whether or not to accept the piece of property, and

b) if he does accept it, how much credit to give you for it. You will have to negotiate the value of the mortgaged property.

Selling Buildings

If you need more cash than you can get from selling or mortgaging an unimproved property (a piece of property that has no houses or hotels on it), you may *sell* a building back to the Bank for one-half its purchase price. Remember, you may not sell or mortgage a piece of property if there are any buildings on it, or if there are buildings on any other properties of that color group. First, dispose of the buildings.

Buildings can only be sold back to the Bank. They cannot be sold to another player. Incidentally, you cannot transfer a building from one of your properties to another, even within the same color group. Once you buy a house or a hotel for a particular property, that building must stay on that property until you return the building to the Bank.

Selling Houses

Houses may be sold back to the Bank at any time, for *one-half* the purchase price. If you paid $150 for a house on Indiana Avenue, the Bank would give you $75 for it. And if you had two houses on Indiana and wanted to sell them both, you would receive a total of $150 for them, even though they cost you a total of $300.

Selling a house is not the same as mortgaging a piece of property. The mortgaged property is still yours. Once you pay back the mortgage and the interest charge, you may turn the Title Deed right side up and begin collecting rent on the property again. But when you sell a house it no longer belongs to you. If you want to construct a house on that same piece of property later on in the game when you've collected some more money, you will have to buy the house at its *original price*—the price listed on the Title Deed. In other words, to reconstruct a house on Indiana Avenue will cost you $150, just as it did when you bought the original house.

All houses on one color group must be sold evenly, one by one. If you start out with:

Pennsylvania Avenue **North Carolina Avenue** **Pacific Avenue**

You have no choice. The first house you sell *must* come from Pennsylvania, to keep the number of houses even. This will leave you with two houses on each property. You may then sell the second house from any of these properties.

Pennsylvania Avenue	**North Carolina Avenue**	**Pacific Avenue**

But you may not sell the next house from Pacific. First, you would have to sell a house from either Pennsylvania or North Carolina—that would leave you with two properties which have one house apiece on them, and a third property which has two houses standing on it.

Pennsylvania Avenue	**North Carolina Avenue**	**Pacific Avenue**

The next time you sell a house from this color group, it must be from Pennsylvania Avenue, to keep the building even.

NOTE: According to the rules of building and selling evenly, you may not have more than a one-house difference between any properties of the same color group.

Selling Hotels

Hotels may be sold back to the Bank at any time for one-half the purchase price. The cost of a hotel equals the cost of five houses. You may sell a hotel (as a last resort) if you need to raise cash, or you may break a hotel down into houses in order to create a building shortage.

If you have a hotel on Kentucky Avenue, you paid

$$
\begin{array}{r}
\$150 \text{ per house} \\
\times \quad 4 \text{ houses} \\
\hline
\$600 \\
+\$150 \text{ (the cost of an additional house)} \\
\hline
\$750 \text{ hotel cost (the equivalent of five houses)}
\end{array}
$$

If you sell this hotel back to the Bank, you will receive one-half of $750, or $375.

Hotels must be sold *evenly*. If you need a lot of money, you may sell all of the hotels on one color group *at the same time*.

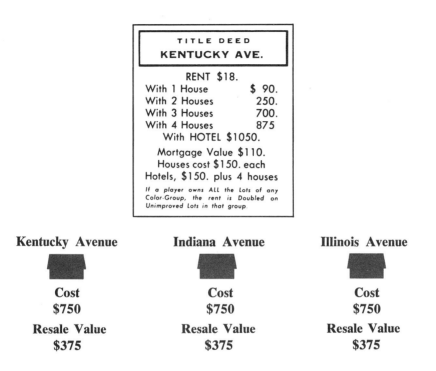

TITLE DEED
KENTUCKY AVE.

RENT $18.
With 1 House $ 90.
With 2 Houses   250.
With 3 Houses   700.
With 4 Houses   875
    With HOTEL $1050.

Mortgage Value $110.
Houses cost $150. each
Hotels, $150. plus 4 houses

If a player owns ALL the Lots of any Color-Group, the rent is Doubled on Unimproved Lots in that group.

Kentucky Avenue	Indiana Avenue	Illinois Avenue
Cost	Cost	Cost
$750	$750	$750
Resale Value	Resale Value	Resale Value
$375	$375	$375

If the Bank has houses available, you have another option. Instead of selling all of the hotels simultaneously, you can convert one or more hotels to houses, and sell the houses one by one—just remember that this must be done evenly.

Suppose, for example, that you own the Yellow building lots—Atlantic Avenue, Ventnor Avenue, and Marvin Gardens—and you have one hotel on each property. You don't want to sell them all, and the Bank has houses available, so:

	Atlantic Avenue	Ventnor Avenue	Marvin Gardens

Legal:

You decide to sell only one house. You keep your hotels on Atlantic Avenue and Marvin Gardens, and you convert the hotel on Ventnor back into houses. Remember, one hotel equals five houses.

Houses on Ventnor cost $150 each. When you sell a house, you receive only one-half the price you paid. So when you return the hotel to the Bank, you receive four houses (which must be placed on Ventnor Avenue in place of the hotel), plus $75.

If that isn't enough, you may need to sell more than one house. You can't sell another from Ventnor—there may not be more than a one-house difference between properties in the same color group. Ventnor now has four houses on it. Atlantic and Marvin each have the equivalent of five houses. Obviously, you'll have to break down another hotel.

If the Bank has enough houses available, you may sell the hotel on Atlantic Avenue and convert it to the equivalent of five houses; you may then sell the fifth house. In other words, you give the Bank your hotel, and the Bank gives you four houses plus $75 (half the purchase price of the "fifth" house).

If you still need more money, you may sell another house, but *not* one from Atlantic or Ventnor! Not, that is, while there is still a hotel on Marvin Gardens. One hotel = five houses. Atlantic Avenue has three houses, leaving a difference of two houses. Remember, the "even" rule says you may not have a difference of more than one house between properties of the same color group.

The only way you could sell another house from this group would be to convert the last hotel into houses. From then on, you could continue to sell the houses evenly.

NOTE: If the Bank does not have enough houses to break down your hotels as you'd like, you must either sell all the buildings from this color group at the same time, or you must convert your hotels to the number of houses that are available.

Suppose you own three hotels on the Yellow lots, and you have to sell three houses. You would have to convert each hotel to four houses; that means you would need twelve houses from the Bank.

What if there are only five houses in the Bank? You could sell your hotels entirely, and have no buildings left on this real estate group. Or you could sell the difference between your hotels and five houses:

$$
\begin{aligned}
3 \text{ hotels} \times 5 \text{ houses each} = 15 &\text{ houses (equivalent)} \\
- 5 &\text{ houses (available from the Bank)} \\
\hline
10 &\text{ houses you would have to sell}
\end{aligned}
$$

If you sell ten houses:

$$
\begin{aligned}
\$ 150 &\text{ original house cost} \\
\times \quad 10 &\text{ houses} \\
\hline
\$1500 &\text{ original cost for 10 houses}
\end{aligned}
$$

Divide the original cost by one-half ($750 cash), which the Bank will give you for the ten houses. The Bank will also give you the five houses, which you must put back onto the Yellow building lots to replace the hotels. Remember to place them evenly. For instance:

	Atlantic Avenue	Ventnor Avenue	Marvin Gardens
Illegal:	🏠🏠🏠	🏠	🏠
Legal:	🏠🏠	🏠🏠	🏠

69

Jail

It's not very hard to get into Jail. All you have to do is:

a) land on the space marked Go to Jail.

b) draw the Chance or Community Chest card marked Go to Jail.

c) throw doubles three times in a row during the course of one turn.

Getting out of Jail is, naturally, somewhat more difficult. First, there is the matter of *when* you can get out.

In being sent to Jail, you have used up your turn. The moment your token lands behind that barred window, your turn ends. You must spend the night, or at least the next round, peering out between the bars while the dice pass from one opponent to the next. When they finally land back in your hand, it is time for your first attempt to gain freedom.

You may get out of Jail on your first turn by

a) using a Get Out of Jail, Free card, if you have one. Just show the card, turn it over and place it beneath the Chance/Community Chest deck, move your token out of Jail onto the Just Visiting area, and throw the dice. Then move forward the indicated number of spaces.

b) purchasing a Get Out of Jail, Free card from another player, and using it as indicated above.

c) paying a fine of $50. Pay the money to the Bank, move your token onto the Just Visiting area, throw the dice, and move your token the proper number of spaces.

d) throwing doubles. If you succeed in throwing doubles on your first try, move your token out of Jail and forward the indicated number of spaces. Even though you have thrown doubles, you do *not* get a second turn. Once you have moved, the turn passes to the next player.

If you haven't managed your great escape this turn, don't worry. You still have two more chances. If you didn't have, couldn't get, or didn't want to use a Get Out of Jail, Free card, and you didn't want to pay the $50, and you tried but failed to throw doubles, your first attempt is over. Give the dice to the next player, and wait until they come around to you again on your second turn, in which you may

a) use a Get Out of Jail, Free card.

b) pay a fine of $50.

c) throw doubles.

If none of these succeeds this time either, you have one last chance to break out. This time, though, your opportunities are a bit more limited. When the dice go around the board for the third time, you can try for one last jailbreak.

On your third turn, you may get out of Jail by

a) using a Get Out of Jail, Free card.

b) paying a fine of $50.

c) throwing doubles.

What? Your third turn has arrived, and you're still not out of Jail? Now wait a minute. The State of Monopoly cannot keep giving you free food and board indefinitely. You cannot stay in Jail any longer.

If you have tried and failed to get out of Jail during three turns, you no longer have any choice. Leave your dice on the table where you threw them during your third turn. Dig into your cashbox and pay the Bank your $50 fine immediately.

If it's your third turn and you must pay the $50 fine to get out of Jail, but you don't have enough money, you must sell or mortgage some buildings or properties to raise the cash. One way or another, you *must* pay this fine, even if it drives you into bankruptcy.

Now, still in your third turn, move your token the number of spaces indicated by the dice you threw a moment ago (when you were still trying to throw doubles). Now you're out. Congratulations.

Other Things About Jail

If you pass GO on your way to Jail, do not collect $200. Technically, when you're sent to Jail, you are supposed to go *directly* there, moving your token in a straight line from wherever it is, right into the Jail. In that case, you don't actually pass GO.

If you are not sent to Jail but just happen, in the course of moving your token around the board, to land on the corner square where the Jail is located, you are "Just Visiting." Your token may remain on the Just Visiting area during that turn, and when the dice come around to you again, just throw them and move as usual.

The State of Monopoly is rather lenient and generous to its convicted criminals. While you are in Jail there, you do not lose your citizenship. You may continue to buy or sell property, buy or sell houses and hotels, and collect rent from anyone who lands on your unmortgaged properties. Just shout out your instructions from your cell.

Any number of players may be in Jail at the same time. Conspiracy, anyone?

COLLECT
$200.00 SALARY
AS YOU PASS

Go

According to the rules, "Each time a player's token lands on or passes over GO, whether by throw of the dice or by drawing a card, the Banker pays him $200 salary. However, $200 is paid only once each time around the board."

A salary is a fixed compensation for services, paid to a person on a regular basis. In Monopoly, that fixed amount is $200—never more, and never less. The service you must perform in order to earn that salary is to move your token forward around the board, in a clockwise direction—that is, in the direction indicated by the arrow on the GO square. Each time you do this, you earn another $200 salary.

If your token is on Pennsylvania Avenue (Green) and you roll a seven, your token would move forward to Mediterranean Avenue, and it would pass GO on the way. The Banker would automatically give you $200. He must; this is not an option. If the Banker isn't looking, by all means wake him up and demand your money. But salary, unlike rent, cannot be forfeited if you wait too long to ask for it. You are legally entitled to your $200, and the Bank must pay it to you.

If you throw a six instead of a seven, your token would land on GO.

The Bank would pay you $200. When it's your turn again, throw the dice and move normally, but do *not* collect another $200. You've already been paid for going around the board this turn.

If your token lands on the Go to Jail square, move your token directly to Jail. Look at the policeman's finger as he points the way: he's not pointing toward GO. He's pointing counterclockwise: backwards. If he sends you to Jail, you do not move your token past GO, so you do not collect $200. If you draw a Chance or Community Chest card that directs you to Go Directly to Jail, the same thing happens. You move directly to Jail. You do not pass GO, and you do not collect $200.

If you pass GO and land on Community Chest or on Chance, you might draw a card telling you to "Advance to GO—Collect $200." Now, how much do you collect? $200 or $400? Let's see.

First you passed GO, which earns you your $200 salary. By a happy coincidence, you landed on Chance or Community Chest, and received instructions to move your token forward around the board to the GO corner. By the time your token reaches GO, you've been around the board again, so you've earned another $200 salary. Your total income for all this rushing around is a cool $400: $200 for each turn.

Income Tax

INCOME
TAX
◆
PAY 10%
OR
$200

The official rules state that, "When a player lands on Income Tax he has two options: he may estimate his tax at $200 and pay the Bank, or he may pay 10 percent of his total worth to the Bank. His total worth is all his cash on hand, printed prices of mortgaged and unmortgaged properties, and cost price of all buildings he owns. The player must decide which option he will take *before* he adds up his total worth."

Last things first. The rule says that if you land on Income Tax, you must decide whether you want to pay the flat $200, or 10 percent of your total worth *before* you calculate how much you own. This means that you should maintain a fairly good idea of your net worth at all times, or tally it up every once in a while as a precaution.

If you decide to pay 10 percent of your total worth, compute your assets by adding the total of:

a) all your money.

b) the cost price of your buildings (the amount of money you paid for them; a hotel costs the price of five houses).

c) the purchase price of all your unmortgaged properties.

d) the mortgage value of all your mortgaged properties.

Then take this total and multiply by .10 to get the amount you must pay the tax man. If your total assets are

$$\begin{array}{r} \$\ \ 750 \\ \times\ \ \ \ .10 \\ \hline \$75.00 \ \text{tax} \end{array}$$

If your total assets are
$$\begin{array}{r} \$\ \ 4382 \\ \times\ \ \ \ .10 \\ \hline \$438.20 \ \text{your tax is \$438} \end{array}$$

If your total assets are
$$\begin{array}{r} \$\ \ 2000 \\ \times\ \ \ \ .10 \\ \hline \$200.00 \ \text{your tax is an even \$200} \end{array}$$

FREE PARKING

Free Parking

The rules state quite clearly that "A player landing on this space does not receive any money, property or reward of any kind. This is just a 'free' resting place."

If you're like many players, you'll remember playing slightly differently. One of the most common variations on the basic Monopoly rules is to place all the money paid for luxury tax, income tax, building repairs, and fines underneath the Free Parking square. The player who lands on the square receives whatever money is there at the time.

This, however, is not a part of the actual rules, and never was. Free Parking is, technically, simply a free space. During the latter part of the game, when the board is dotted with expensive houses and hotels, it can be a great relief to land on Free Parking instead of on your opponent's urban development.

If you want to play with the variation to this rule, make sure you announce your house rules at the beginning of the game, and be certain each player understands and approves of any changes you're making in the official rules.

Bankruptcy

"A player is bankrupt when he owes more than he can pay either to another player or to the Bank." (Official rules, page 143, paragraph 2.)

If your debts have gotten out of hand, you may try to salvage the situation by doing some fast negotiating with your creditor or with a third party. If nothing works, you must liquidate your assets.

Trying to Avoid Bankruptcy

If you owe money to the Bank, because of a huge tax, fine, or building repairs bill, you must pay the amount in full. The Bank does not make deals. Your first procedure in trying to raise cash must be the sale of your buildings back to the Bank for one-half their purchase price. Once your properties are vacant lots again, figure out how much you would get if you mortgage them. Still not enough? If you're lucky, or have a friendly opponent, you may be able to get another player to buy some of your properties, and your Get Out of Jail, Free card for a price that would give you enough money to pay the debt. You may not sell to another player, however, unless you would wind up with the full amount of money that you owe. In other words, you cannot sell your properties for cheap prices in order to help a particular opponent and, at the same time, cheat your creditor. If you're offered a price which will still leave you short of the amount you owe, you cannot go through with the sale. Your properties must be turned over to the Bank in lieu of your payment, and you are out of the game.

If you owe money to an opponent, you may try to make a deal in which your creditor will take some or all of your undeveloped property (with no houses or hotels on it) as payment of your debt. If your creditor refuses, you may try to sell properties to another player, but you may only do this if you will wind up with enough money to pay your creditor in full.

Liquidating: Going into Bankruptcy

If you cannot raise enough money to pay your debts, you must declare yourself bankrupt. First, sell all your buildings back to the Bank for one-half their cost price.

If your debt is to another player, you must then turn over all your remaining assets—money, mortgaged and unmortgaged properties—to that player. Your creditor must accept all of your assets, including mortgaged properties, as part of his payment.

If you give a creditor a mortgaged property, he has two choices: he may pay the Bank the 10 percent interest charge plus the mortgage price, and lift the mortgage immediately. Or he may pay the Bank only the 10 percent interest charge, and keep the property mortgaged for awhile. If he chooses the latter course, he must pay the Bank an *additional 10 percent* when he finally lifts the mortgage.

If your debt is to the Bank, once you've sold your buildings you must turn over all of your mortgaged and unmortgaged properties and the remainder of your cash. The Bank immediately auctions off whatever properties you've given it, at the regular (unmortgaged) price. A mortgaged property sold by auction to another player is no longer considered mortgaged. The new owner may start collecting rent on the property immediately.

As soon as your assets are all gone, you must retire from the game.

NOTE: In liquidating your assets, if you have a Get Out of Jail, Free card, return it face down to the bottom of the appropriate deck. The card has no monetary worth.

Variations

Now that we've finished establishing the rules, here are some ways to break them. Playing Monopoly seems to become a very personal thing. Many people develop their own set of house rules which they adhere to as rigidly and steadfastly as if they were law. Some of these variations are regional, some exist only in the minds of the occupants of a particular household, but some variations are fairly common, played by many people throughout the country —or maybe the world.

Here are a few of the most prevalent deviations. Try them in your own game, and see if you like them. You may even be surprised to find some of them familiar. Many players become so used to playing with their particular variation that they assume it's part of the normal rules of the game.

NOTE: One of the most frequent causes of disputes in play comes about when variations are used that have not been completely established beforehand. However you decide to play, if you make any change in the basic, official rules be certain to discuss all of the changes and *their related ramifications* before the game actually begins. Be aware that some seemingly innocent changes may have far-reaching effects. If you create variations of your own, try to anticipate "but what happens if . . . " kinds of situations. For instance, if your variation involves ownership (sharing, partnership, joint tenancy or whatever) of a property or color group, what happens if that property must be sold or mortgaged? Etc., etc., etc. Some variations can cause immense headaches.

But don't let that stop you. In the highly unlikely event that you find basic Monopoly becoming a bit tedious, be creative. Try a variation. Like one of these:

The Free Parking Jackpot

At the beginning of the game, the Bank puts a $500 bill under Free Parking. In practice, some people place a corner of the money under the Free Parking corner of the board, with the rest of the bill sticking out. Some put the money on top of the Free Parking square. And many people have a Free Parking area on the board itself, next to the squares on which the Chance and Community Chest cards sit. (Just leave room to throw the dice.)

As the game progresses, money is added to the Free Parking pot every time a player pays a fine, a tax, or a building or street repairs bill. In other words, all the money which, in a normal game, would be paid to the Bank now goes to Free Parking. (Exceptions: money for the purchase of properties or buildings, or for the mortgaging of properties or the sale of buildings, goes to the Bank as usual.)

Example: money you pay for landing on Luxury Tax or Income Tax goes into the Free Parking pot. So does the money you pay if a Chance or Community Chest card directs you to pay a poor tax, or if you are assessed for street repairs ("Pay $25 for each house and $40 for each hotel.")

Every time a player *lands on* Free Parking, he collects whatever money is in the pot at that time.

NOTE: The Bank does *not* replace the $500 bill after the first Free Parking jackpot is collected. This is merely a bonus for the first player lucky enough to land there.

Maximum Punishment

In normal Monopoly, a jailed player retains his citizenship. In this variation, all of his rights and privileges are suspended until he completes serving his sentence.

While in Jail, a player cannot collect rent on his properties. He cannot buy, sell, trade, or mortgage properties or buildings.

All of his rights are restored to him once he regains his status as a free citizen.

GO to GO

Under the normal rules, when a player lands *on* GO he collects the usual salary of $200. He does not collect a second time when, on his next turn, he moves his token past GO and onto the first side of the board.

In this variation, a player collects *$400* if he lands on the GO square. As with the normal game, he does not collect again on his next turn.

NOTE: A player whose token *passes* GO, but does not land directly on it, collects the normal $200. Going to GO on orders from a Chance or Community Chest card, you collect the normal $200, according to the instructions on the card.

Doubling Up

Normally, any number of tokens may occupy the same square. In this variation, a square may only be occupied by one token at a time. If your token happens to land on an occupied square (a square on which another token is standing), you must move your token *backwards* to GO. Do not collect any salary when you get there; this is a punishment, not a reward. On your next turn, simply throw the dice and move as usual.

NOTE: If another player is in Jail and you land on Just Visiting, your token can remain there. This corner counts, in effect, as two spaces. Any number of players can be in Jail simultaneously, and more than one player may occupy the GO square.

Immunity

One player may agree to grant another player full or partial immunity from paying rent on one or more of his properties. If Player Three owns Boardwalk and you trade him Park Place, so that he now owns the Dark Blues, he may, as part of your trading agreement, grant you rent-free passage over his territory no matter how many buildings he puts on it. With such a grant of immunity, you may safely land on either Park Place or Boardwalk. Even if both properties have hotels on them, you would pay no rent.

The specific terms of immunity can vary according to the deal you make with your opponent. Player Three may grant you full immunity on the Dark Blues; thereafter, for the rest of the game *or until Player Three sells or trades those properties,* you pay no rent if you land on them.

You may make a lesser deal and get some kind of partial or temporary immunity. According to the agreement you reach, this would allow you to:

a) pay full rent on Boardwalk, but no rent on Park Place.

b) pay full rent on both properties as long as they remain undeveloped, but no rent once buildings have been constructed.

c) pay no rent only the first time you land on either property, but full rent thereafter.

d) or any variation on this theme.

When *you* gain immunity on Player Three's Dark Blue properties, it has no effect on any other player. Player Two, for example, must pay full rent to Player Three if he lands on Boardwalk. Your immunity on these particular properties has no bearing on any other properties on the board. You do not have to pay rent for landing on Boardwalk, but if you land on Marvin Gardens, full rent would be due, even if Marvin also belongs to Player Three.

You can have immunity on several different properties belonging to one player, or on different properties belonging to different players. But at the time you negotiate for your immunity, be sure to arrange what will happen if the property changes hands. Generally, the immunity agreement does not extend to the new landlord. Convention also forbids double-trading: Player Three trades the properties to Player Two, and they subsequently trade back again. Player Three has thus reacquired the Dark Blues, but you have lost your immunity. Whatever agreements you reach beforehand must be binding throughout the game.

Short Monopoly

Remember that Parker Brothers has developed its own variations. There are two of them printed on your set of rules (see Appendix), which explain methods of playing shorter, limited-time versions of the basic game.

3
Strategy
and Tactics

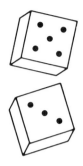

Basic Principles

Monopoly is a game of luck and skill. The roll of the dice can make or break you, sometimes in one turn. It's delightful to land on an unowned property, buy it, and so own a complete color group on which you can now build costly houses and hotels. It is equally delightful to land on an unowned property which your opponent dearly wants—perhaps it would complete a valuable group he has been accumulating. And it is devastating to flick your wrist, release the dice, and see them fall on a number that would land your token on Income Tax, or worse yet, on a well-developed property which belongs to your opponent.

At such times, it is perfectly acceptable to rise with dignity, hand over your losses, sigh gently, and speculate on the caprices of the gods of fortune.

But there is much more to Monopoly than luck alone. Played correctly, within the obviously uncontrollable limits imposed by chance, the skillful player can manipulate many situations to his advantage, utilize opportunities another might ignore, and generally outwit his opponent—with at least a minimum of cooperation from the dice.

The object of Monopoly is to become the richest player on the board in terms of total assets—cash, property, and buildings—and to drive all of your opponents into bankruptcy. How? In large part, by combining your luck and skill to acquire property, and then erecting houses and hotels on these properties to make them more expensive, thus creating high-rent districts which your opponents cannot afford to land on.

But which are the best properties to buy? What are the best times to build? When should you hoard a large cash reserve? How can you weaken your opponent's holdings? And, among the most important factors, how can you make the most successful property trades? These are matters of strategy and skill.

Obviously, to win the game you've got to make your money work for you. Hiding it under a mattress will give you a handy reserve with which to pay your rent whenever your token lands on your opponent's increasingly expensive properties, but eventually the money pile will run out, and even the $200 salary you get each time you pass GO will not be enough to meet your expenses. You've got to bring money *in* in large amounts. The best way to do that, of course, is to develop complete color groups, and then put houses and hotels on them.

There are several major points to remember, though, before deciding which properties to go after, and where to build first (assuming you have a choice). These points are listed below, then explained in detail.

1. You must be aware of the *return on your investment*. That is, how *profitable* is a particular piece of property or property group? Suppose someone offered to sell you a gold mine with a guaranteed gross income of one million dollars per year. Sounds great, doesn't it? But what if it costs you ten million dollars to buy it? Now it begins to look like a losing investment, at least for the first ten years.

But suppose you were offered a silver mine, with a guaranteed fifty thousand dollar annual income. A paltry sum, hardly worth considering— except when you hear that the asking price is twenty thousand dollars. You'd make back your purchase price plus a profit of thirty thousand dollars your first year!

2. You must be aware of *the amount of money you have available for investment*. Let's examine three hypothetical taxicab owners:

Mr. Rich buys a luxurious, new taxicab, which costs him a fortune, because it will last him for many years with a minimum of maintenance and repair bills. Over the long run, it will save him money and help him become even richer.

Mr. Poor buys an old, used taxicab, which costs him very little, because very little is all the money he has. He knows that his cheaper car will not last as long and will need more frequent repairs than Mr. Rich's car, but as long as he can keep the used cab running, Mr. Poor will be earning money. Maybe, someday, he'll even earn enough to buy a shiny, new cab.

Mr. Foolish has enough money to pay cash for a used taxicab, but he has his heart set on getting a brand new cab immediately. So he buys one on credit. True, his new cab will help him earn money, but the interest payments will use up most of his profits.

What have taxicabs to do with Monopoly? Not very much. But the concept of expensive properties versus cheap properties is crucial. You can make money from either, if you invest in them properly, and if you bear in mind —before rushing out to buy that house—how much money you have available to build up a particular color group.

3. You must be aware of the probability of *how frequently your opponent will land on your property.* Even if you have one of the most valuable properties on the board, which will give you the best return on your investment, and you have just the right amount of money to develop it to its most profitable level, the amount of money you make from that property will depend, in large part, on how often your opponent's token lands on it.

The trick to successful Monopoly investing is to combine these three factors. The financial factors are, in fact, inextricably interconnected. Obviously, building a hotel anywhere on the board is a good and profitable idea. In fact, acquiring and setting up buildings on your properties should be one of your primary goals in the game. The more the merrier. (Your other major goal should be the acquisition of more color groups, so that you can build even more houses and hotels. As I said, the more the merrier.)

You will have to start at the beginning, though, and this is the point at which decisions—strategy—can be crucial. Examine your situation, appraise your cash and property, see what your opponent has (and figure out what *his* strategy will be), and make some plans. Which color groups will you go after first?

The Low Rent Group
Mediterranean and Baltic
Oriental, Vermont, Connecticut

The Middle Rent Group
St. Charles, States, Virginia
St. James, Tennessee, New York

The Upper-Middle Rent Group
Kentucky, Indiana, Illinois
Atlantic, Ventnor, Marvin Gardens

The High Rent Group
Pacific, North Carolina, Pennsylvania
Park Place and Boardwalk

How to Decide Which Property Group to Develop

To make your decision, first consider:

a) your available cash, and then

b) compare the relative return on your investment between the color groups available to you.

Let's look at two obvious, and opposite examples to see how the size of your bankroll affects where you should build. The Green color group—Pacific, North Carolina and Pennsylvania Avenues—costs a total of $920 to buy. Houses cost $200 apiece to construct. If you want to put one house on each of the Greens, it would cost you (including property cost) a total of $1,520. Divide that by three to get the average price for a Green building lot with one house, and the result is roughly $505. That's a pretty hefty amount. If the rent you collect as a result is high enough, the investment is well worth it. But is it?

87

Green properties with one house rent for $130, $130 and $150 respectively for an average rent of $137. Let's call it $135.

Divide the rent into the cost: $135 $\overline{)505}$ = 3.74

Divide 3.74 into 100 percent and you get roughly 26.7 percent return on your investment.

Is that good or bad, you ask? The only way to tell is by making a comparison. The Light Blue color group—Oriental, Vermont, and Connecticut Avenues—costs a total of $320 to buy. Houses cost $50 apiece to construct. To put one house on each of the Light Blues would cost you (including property cost) a total of $470. Divide that by three, and the average price for a Light Blue building lot with one house is $157 (approximately).

Light Blues with one house have an average rent of $33 apiece.

Divide the rent into the cost: $33 $\overline{)157.00}$ = 4.76

Divide 4.76 into 100 percent and you get roughly 21 percent return on your investment.

Now, for those of you who prefer Monopoly as a game instead of a mathematical exercise, what does all this mean, anyway?

Look closely at the results for just a moment, and you'll see.

ONE HOUSE ON EACH PROPERTY

	Total Investment	Average Rent	Percentage of Return on Investment
Green color group	$1520	$135	26.7%
Light Blue color group	$ 470	$ 33	21.0%

The returns on your investments—a way of measuring the amount of profit you're actually making—are remarkably similar: 26.7 percent compared with 21.0 percent. Yet the amount of initial investment required to earn those returns is radically different: $1520 compared with $470! Without going into all the calculations, here's what happens if you build *two* houses on each of the Light Blue properties, compared with only *one* house on each of the Greens:

ONE HOUSE PER GREEN PROPERTY
TWO HOUSES PER LIGHT BLUE PROPERTY

	Total Investment	Average Rent	Percentage of Return on Investment
Green color group	$1520	$135	26.7%
Light Blue color group	$ 620	$ 93	45.2%

Now the comparison is even more startling. With the same investment in the Greens, and only a slight increase in investment in the Light Blues, the percentage of returns has become radically different. At this point, the purchase of two houses on each property of the Light Blues is *much* more profitable than the purchase of one house apiece on the Greens, and yet it has cost you only a fraction of the Green price!

Do you want to see this carried to the extreme? At $50 per house, it costs $250 to buy a hotel on each Light Blue property. Three hotels would cost you $750. Including your property cost of $320, you've now spent $1070, and you get a whopping 159 percent return on your investment.

ONE HOUSE PER GREEN PROPERTY
ONE HOTEL PER LIGHT BLUE PROPERTY

	Total Investment	Average Rent	Percentage of Return on Investment
Green color group	$1520	$135	26.7%
Light Blue color group	$1070	$567	159.0%

In other words, if you choose to buy three hotels for your Light Blues, instead of three houses (one per property) for your Greens, *you will invest only one-third the amount of money, and you will earn a return of almost six times as much.*

Does this mean that the Light Blue group is better to own and develop than the Green lots? Not necessarily. The percentage of return on your investment increases greatly for the Greens if you can afford to buy at least three houses on each property.

The whole point is: *how much money do you have to invest in buildings?* While there are exceptions to this rule, by and large your guiding principle should be:

If you have only a small amount of cash, use it to construct buildings on the low income properties.

If you have a large amount of cash, use it to develop your high income groups.

The following chart indicates which properties are your best investments, depending on the amount of money you have to invest in and develop them. As you can see, there are various alternatives in investing your money well, but the best returns come from investing this way:

Most Profitable Property Investments Per Dollars Invested	
Amount of Money Available	Best Investment (in order of best returns)
(With the exception of the Railroads, "investment" means buying buildings.)	
Below $500	Railroads
$500	Purple
From $500 to $700	Light Blue
From $800 to $1000	Orange/Maroon
From $1100 to $1500	Orange/Maroon/Dark Blue/Yellow/Red
From $1600 to $2000	Dark Blue/Yellow/Red/Green
From $2100 to $2500	Yellow/Red/Green
From $2500 to $3000	Green

How Many Buildings?

If you have more than one color group, *develop one group at a time, up to its optimum level.* You've already decided which to start building on first. Stick with that group until it's paying the highest percentage of return on your investment.

The relative cost of improving building lots differs from property to property. Yet each property, or color group, tends to have a most profitable point. The problem is to find it and take advantage of it.

Just for fun, compare the different returns you get if you own Mediterranean and Baltic Avenues. Each property costs $60 to buy. A hotel on each costs an additional $250, for a total investment of $310. Yet compare their relative earning powers:

	Total Cost	Rent	Percentage of Return on Investment
Mediterranean Avenue	$310	$250	80.6%
Baltic Avenue	$310	$450	145.2%

Unfortunately, the build even rule makes it impossible for you to construct a hotel on Baltic Avenue without building at least four houses on Mediterranean. But you do have a choice as to which color group to invest your hard-earned money in. If you're fortunate enough—or shrewd enough—to acquire more than one complete color group, consider carefully which to develop and *how much to develop it* in order to get the best return on your investment—that is, to get the most for your money.

The biggest increase comes with the purchase of the third house. Once you have developed your properties this far, they begin paying a good return on your investment. The general rule of thumb, then, is to develop each color group until you have at least three houses on each property of that group. Then you can turn your attention to developing your other properties. 91

Develop First and Fast

It is important to note that the first person to have a *highly developed* color group gets an enormous headstart on driving his opponents into bankruptcy. He doesn't necessarily win, but, with some luck, his opponents will land on his building development, incur his high rentals, and lose the cash reserves they need to develop their own urban centers.

? The Facts of Probability

In Monopoly, the dice determine, to a great extent, which properties you (and your opponents) are likely to land on. There are several other factors, however, that exert considerable influence. If you land on Chance or Community Chest, you could draw a card that would require you to move your token to a different square. And the possibility of landing in Jail makes certain sides of the board more likely to be landed on, and certain areas very unlikely to be landed on.

Professor Irvin R. Hentzel, a mathematician, programmed all these factors into a computer and came up with the following list. The most frequently landed on squares are:

Illinois Avenue
GO
B&O Railroad
Free Parking
Tennessee Avenue
New York Avenue
Reading Railroad
St. James Place
Water Works
Pennsylvania Railroad

The properties on this list automatically increase in value, since it is more probable that they will be landed on often, and yield their rent more frequently. Keep this list in mind when you're considering buying, trading, mortgaging or building on these properties or their related properties (in terms of color groups, Railroads, and Utilities).

With the exception of the Reading Railroad, all the properties on the list are located on the second and third sides of the board. (The Reading draws a lot of traffic partially because it's right near GO, and partially because there are two different types of cards which send tokens to it: "Take a ride on the Reading" and "Advance token to the nearest Railroad.") It is no coincidence that the most frequently landed-on sides of the board are those just past Jail. The probabilities of spending time in Jail are rather high. You can land your token on the Go to Jail square, or draw a Go Directly to Jail card from either the Chance or the Community Chest decks, or simply have the misfortune to roll three doubles in a row. When you're finally released, your throw of the dice must land you on either the second (the Maroon and Orange) or the third (the Red and the Yellow) side of the board. The properties that lie on these sides thus get a lot of rent-paying traffic, which makes them very valuable. In addition, many players get out of Jail by rolling doubles. Properties that are an even number of squares (from two to twelve) past Jail are thus particularly likely to be landed on.

Probable Dice Throws

The most commonly thrown total is seven, and you have a one-in-six chance of rolling it. Other totals become less probable as they get farther away from seven in either direction. Your chances of throwing either a six or an eight, for example, are five out of thirty-six, while your chances of throwing either a two or a twelve are only one out of thirty-six.

If you really like to calculate the odds of your opponent's landing on your brand new hotel (or of your landing on his!), here's how the chances break down:

Total of Throw (both dice)	Probability
a 2 or a 12	1/36
a 3 or an 11	2/36 (1/18)
a 4 or a 10	3/36 (1/12)
a 5 or a 9	4/36 (1/9)
a 6 or an 8	5/36
a 7	6/36 (1/6)

Specific Strategies and Tactics

Now that you know the basic principles involved in the game, you can adopt your own system of strategies and tactics to develop your own winning style of play.

Some of the methods and techniques discussed here should be kept in mind as you play. Others apply only at specific times, or in certain situations. If you've been playing the game, you may find that you've been doing some of these things without knowing why. Examine them now to see how to use each of these systems in the most effective way possible, so that you can increase your wealth and drive your opponents into ruin and bankruptcy.

The Prince or the Pauper

One day I sat on a park bench and watched a wiry little lady selling flowers. She did a brisk business; it was one of the first warm days of spring, and people were out tasting the inviting air of the new season. A squirrel darted by and caught my attention for a while, and when I remembered to look back at the flower lady, she was just selling her last bunch of carnations. Pocketing her silver, she stooped, gathered up her empty carton, and trundled off down the path toward the street. That seemed to signal the end of the afternoon, so I got up and went on my way—which, by chance, happened to lead down the same path. I emerged on the street to find the little flower lady standing beside a gleaming new Cadillac Eldorado. A young man emerged from the car, kissed her on the cheek, and asked: "Hi, Mom. How's it going today?" She told him it was going just fine, and waited while he replaced her empty box with a full one, heaped with bunches of colorful flowers. As he started to help her carry the box back down the path, she stopped him impatiently. The day was far too nice to waste any time! She could carry the box herself; he should drive several blocks to where another flower seller was working (I imagined a wiry little man), and unload the rest of the flowers that were in the car. Then they were both to rejoin her in an hour. Business was going so well, she thought she'd break early today. The wiry little lady watched the young man drive off in what was obviously *her* gleaming new Cadillac Eldorado, then lifted the box of flowers, grunted, and turned back down the path.

In other words, there are many ways to get rich.

The most important strategic decision you must make is whether to be a prince or a pauper. These are not end results; they reflect the way you will start the game, the underlying attitude which will determine many of your actions. As you have seen, the most profitable way to invest your money is to focus on a particular group of properties and develop them until they are paying you a profitable return. You must decide, as early as possible in the game, which color group you intend to develop first—and then go to it.

If you decide to develop an inexpensive block of real estate, you will use the pauper's attack. If you decide to develop an expensive color group, you will follow the strategy of the prince's restraint. With luck and skill, they're both successful methods of getting rich, sooner or later.

The Pauper's Attack

Once you've gone around the board a few times and have begun to accumulate some property, sit back, look around the table (or floor), and take stock of who has what. By now, the Bank should have sold quite a few Title

Deeds, and several players should be well on their way toward collecting interesting real estate. If there are several of you playing, it will be difficult for anyone to acquire a complete color group by the luck of landing on each of the properties of that group. Some trading will be necessary, and there are few absolute rules as to which properties to trade away and which to try to buy. It depends on the circumstances of each specific game.

By this point, some patterns should have established themselves. Each of you started out with $1500. How much cash have you managed to save? How about your opponents? Which properties have you bought? What does each of your opponents own? Which strategy do you think it will be easier for you to play at this point: the pauper, or the prince?

The pauper's attack requires less of a monetary investment, and it does not pay off with enormous rentals. It does, however, give you a very early return on your money: you start bringing in decent rents in the early part of the game. It has several advantages, therefore: you can become a pauper without too much money (and near the beginning of the game, this is the normal situation), and you can, with a bit of luck, prevent your opponent from accumulating enough cash to develop his own property. If this situation continues long enough it may not actually win the game for you (the $200 he gets each time he passes GO may prevent him from going bankrupt), but it may get you into a position wherein you can make a major investment in a more expensive color group, which you could then develop quickly. That could be the final straw to wipe out your opposition.

To play the pauper's attack, choose a property group that pays off well with a minimum of investment. The Orange group is ideal, but the Maroon works well, too. Both yield excellent returns on investments of $800 to $1,500. The Light Blues are a possibility for this strategy if you happen to own them. They aren't as frequently landed on, however, and won't accomplish the purpose as neatly of depleting your opponent's cash reserves. The Purple pair draws in a minimal income and is only landed on rarely. Oddly enough, the Dark Blue group works well in a pauper's strategy. Because it has only two properties, even though houses are extremely expensive, you can achieve a decent amount of development for a reasonable amount of money. For $1,200 (housing cost), you can erect three houses on each lot and get an excellent return on your money.

The whole key to success with this strategy is to *build early*. Devote all your cash to this purpose, and do whatever you can to raise more cash quickly. If you don't get those buildings up fast, your opponent will save enough money to develop his own more expensive properties, and, once his rentals exceed yours, forget it.

You probably won't have enough money to buy your minimum of three houses on each building lot of the color group you're developing. If you do have that much cash, perhaps you should be playing the prince's restraint. To raise the additional funds, mortgage other properties to the Bank, sell your Get Out of Jail, Free cards, and even consider selling or trading other properties.

If you can manage to acquire the four Railroads *extremely* early in the game, they can support your strategy admirably. First of all, they are a constant drain on your not-yet-rich opponent, and that constant $200 rent at this point will be both harmful and annoying, especially as he's bound to land on one or another Railroad fairly frequently. Let him ride the rails enough to become sufficiently annoyed at the very thought of taking another trip, then offer to trade all four for one of his inexpensive or middle-priced property groups. By that time, he'll probably be delighted to swap either the Light Blues or the Maroons, or possibly even the Oranges (if you've applied a bit of verbal psychology). If you've carefully hoarded the train fares he's been paying you, you should now have enough money to construct houses on the new color group right away, and the higher property rents you'll collect will more than make up for the $200 fare you'll now have to pay him when you yourself take a train ride.

One of the best ways of raising instant cash is to *sell* real estate. If you own both the Greens and the Oranges, for instance, and your opponent has managed to get hold of the Maroon group, offer to trade him the Green lots for $1,000 in cash plus his Maroon group. He may rant and rage and call your offer ridiculous, and maybe he'll bargain you down to the Maroon properties plus only $900, but deep in his conniving heart he'll be rejoicing at what he thinks is a supreme error. Most people consider the Green properties to be the most valuable property on the board, and this is correct— if you're in a position to develop them properly. They only bring in a high rent because it costs so much to build houses and hotels on them.

So there's your opponent, chortling at your folly and gleefully fondling the pretty Green Title Deeds that he now has little money to develop. You, on the other hand, can afford some inward chortling of your own. You have managed to acquire the kind of money that can make your Orange properties really pay off, and if you need more development money you can even mortgage the Maroon properties. But don't build on them, remember, until your Orange group is a minor Levittown, with at least three houses on each lot.

The Prince's Restraint

This strategy seems a bit riskier than the pauper's attack, since your more expensive properties don't pay off until later on in the game; but when they pay off, the profits are high and the damage to an opponent can be fatal.

In the prince's restraint, you put your all into an expensive color group— the Green is best, but even the Yellow does well for this. Because houses are so expensive here, you should only take this route if you already have a good deal of cash and expect to come into some more. But even with a lot of money to start with, it's going to cost you $1,800 (housing cost) just to construct three houses on each Green lot, or $1,350 for three houses on each Yellow. Obviously, then, it's going to take a while to amass enough capital to buy enough houses to make this property pay off. In the meantime, you must have some other way to keep yourself solvent. It helps if you hold the final card in your opponents' color groups, or if they are preventing one another from getting complete groups. That way, you'll never have to pay them high rentals, while you're trying to develop your own building complex.

If your opponent has a complete property group, it can devastate your plan if he develops it too much. Paying him rent on even inexpensive properties when there are two or three (or more) houses standing on them will drain your precious resources and you'll never accumulate enough money to make your own properties profitable. Since it's illegal to steal or set fire to his money to prevent him from building, you must use psychology to convince him how foolish he would be to buy houses at this crucial point in the game. After all, you might mention casually, it's always necessary to maintain a large cash reserve. Everyone knows that. Drop some sage advice, like how important it is to build houses toward the end of the game, as you yourself intend to do. But never early in the game; it ties up one's cash reserves.

Make it stick by adhering to your own advice, especially if your impertinent opponent doubts your word and constructs a few houses. Curl your lip and sit quietly as he sets them down on his cheap lots. Glance coolly and significantly at your own expensive real estate and at your visible bankroll. Then shrug your shoulders and continue the play without doing any buying of your own. This may make him wonder about his own business acumen, and could help prevent him from future buying impulses while you continue to build your capital. What your opponent may not understand is that for you to construct one or two houses would be a losing proposition. They would not draw in enough rent to offset their cost. In your high-rent district, housing costs are so high that, ideally, it doesn't pay to build any houses unless you can build many all at once.

In fact, if you're really set on trying this strategy, you might spend your time accumulating money even before you have acquired your complete expensive property group (as long as no one else has it and starts building on it). Once you have enough cash to buy a large number of houses, you can negotiate a trade for the properties you need and develop them all at once. The princely strategy truly requires restraint.

The Money Method

$ In Monopoly, as in life, your success or failure is dependent, in part, on luck. Being in the right place at the right time—or tossing the "right" number with the fickle dice—is the uncontrollable factor.

But within the limitations of each chance situation are circumstances which you can affect through deliberation and intent. You can make the most of each situation, you can let potentially good opportunities slip by, or you can foul them up. It all depends on your skill in planning successful strategies, and on the tactics you use in implementing them.

The old adage says "Money comes to money." Almost, but not quite. Money is not inherently magnetic—it depends on what you *do* with it.

The object of Monopoly is to become rich. Please note: wealth is not measured simply by totaling the piles of bills neatly arrayed before you. Wealth consists, as well, of your other assets: your properties and your buildings.

In the game of Monopoly, there are three ways you can get money:

a) you collect a salary of $200 each time your token passes GO. (This payment is not optional. The Bank *must* disperse this money to each player as soon as his token *lands on or passes over* the GO square.)

b) you may, by luck, land on either Chance or Community Chest and draw a card which instructs you to receive a certain sum. In most cases such as "You have won second prize in a beauty contest. Collect $10." or "Xmas fund matures. Collect $100." you will be paid by the Bank. Only when a card specifically stipulates otherwise ("Collect $50 from each player ") will this money be paid to you by your opponent.

c) you can collect money if an opponent lands on an unmortgaged property which belongs to you. The amount he must pay will depend on how many properties you own within that particular property group or on how many and what kind of buildings you have erected on that building lot.

Here are some specific techniques, both good and bad, that can affect your attempt at accumulating cash:

The Premature Development Risk

The premature development error occurs if you spend your money to buy property or, more probably, to erect buildings, without enough regard to the fact that your opponent has well-developed properties upon which you might land. You thus leave yourself cash-poor and in trouble if you land on one of these built-up properties.

To build or not to build is a question of delicate timing. Early in the game, the general rule is to build quickly. But as play progresses and green and red roofs begin to dot the board, you have to use some prudence in deciding when to erect more roofs of your own.

In general, it's nicest to leave yourself enough cash so that you can pay any rental charges you may incur. This, of course, is the ideal. At the very least, however, you should—whenever possible—have enough resources so that the sum total of your cash-on-hand, plus the cash you can raise from mortgaging *undeveloped properties* (building lots with no houses or hotels on them), will enable you to pay the highest rent on the board.

Always avoid selling buildings back to the Bank! You lose half the cost of each building, and this money is not recoverable. In mortgaging a lot, you borrow one-half of the property value from the Bank, and repay this loan, plus 10 percent interest, when you lift the mortgage. You do lose the interest, but that's a reasonable amount—especially compared to current "real bank" interest rates. (It's interesting to speculate on Charles Darrow's foresight. Remember, he invented Monopoly in 1933!)

Obviously, the need to maintain a cash reserve must be balanced against the advantage you can gain by improving your property. In deciding if you can afford to buy buildings now, consider:

a) your opponent's most expensive rental.

b) your cash on hand.

c) your undeveloped properties, in terms of what you have available to mortgage, should the need arise. Remember, mortgage the Utilities first, followed by single color lots. Next, you can decide between a cheap (Purple or

Light Blue) undeveloped group or an isolated Railroad, although I'd mortgage the Railroad first if there's any way of getting the chance to build houses in the near future. Do try to avoid mortgaging building-lot groups: remember, you can't build a house on a property until all the other lots in that color group are unmortgaged.

d) consider your own proximity to your opponent's expensive properties, and his proximity to the lot you're thinking of developing. Estimate both your chances of landing on each other's properties. (See The Facts of Probability, page 92.)

The Monetary Bluff

There are times when it's very important to know how much money your opponent has, and for your opponent to know how much you've got. Suppose he offered you a trade early in the game, and as a result of the trade you would get the Oranges, and he would get the Greens. At the moment, neither of you has any complete color groups, and there are no houses or hotels on the board.

At this point, the amount of cash your opponent has is crucial. It costs $200 to buy one house on the Green lots. If he has at least $600 cash, he could erect one house on each Green property for rents of $130, $130, and $150. It would hurt to land on one of them, but it wouldn't be catastrophic for you. On the other hand, with the higher building and property prices, your opponent would be losing money on his Greens with only one house apiece. Two houses on each Green would cost him $1,200, and he'd collect a top rent of $450 on Pennsylvania; the other two properties rent for $390 apiece. This is more painful for you if you land on a Green, but the return on your opponent's investment is still poor. If, however, your opponent can afford to build *three* houses on his Greens, you'd have a problem. The rent jumps enormously ($900, $900, and $1,000), and so do the profits. Even though you'd lose your own chance to gain a complete color group, if your opponent has enough money to construct three or more houses on the properties he'd gain from your trade, then this is *not* the time to trade!

Now reverse your thinking a bit. Just as it is crucial for you to know your opponent's cash supply, it is equally important for him to know how much money you have, so that he can decide whether or not to trade with you. Knowledge of one another's bankroll can also influence decisions on when to buy and where to invest. Obviously, then, it can be an advantage if your opponent thinks you're poorer than you really are.

The monetary bluff takes advantage of a hole in the Monopoly rules. The rules state very clearly that you must display all your property deeds in front of you, so that they are visible to your opponent. There is no mention made of where to place your money, however. It is generally convenient to have it spread out in front of you, but it needn't *all* be clearly visible. Why not put a $500 bill underneath your pile of $1 bills? Or slide it under your foot? Or someplace more creative? Bluff your opponent into thinking you're a bit cash-poor. It just may influence him into making a decision in your favor.

The Midas Mistake

As soon as houses and hotels start springing up on your opponent's properties, it's helpful to set aside a cash reserve to cover the highest rent you might have to pay. In most cases this means making a choice in what to do with your money. How much do you invest, and how much do you save for a rainy—or high rent—day?

To make this decision, consider your own properties. How much have you developed them? How much more development do they need? What specific property trades should you try to negotiate?

Ideally, you should develop all of your property groups to their most profitable stage. This generally means erecting at least three houses on each building lot. If you have fewer houses on each property, you're losing profit. You can't afford *not* to develop these lots further. If you can, of course, try to develop hotels on each of your properties.

If you own two out of three building lots of a valuable color group—for instance, Illinois and Kentucky Avenues—and your opponent owns Indiana, the third property from that group, it may be time to do some trade negotiating. To complete your grouping, it may be necessary to offer your opponent cash along with a piece of property in order to get him to agree to trade.

The Midas mistake occurs when you're so worried about having money to pay your rent that you hoard too much cash; you underdevelop your own color groups, or neglect to invest in necessary trading to acquire additional properties. This leaves you with a hefty bundle of cash for the moment, but with severely limited means of maintaining your cash supply. Proper investment of your money is your only means of gaining a steady income, and, to a large degree, the more you invest, the higher your potential income. Don't be penny wise and pound foolish. Do, by all means, try to maintain a cash reserve, but don't do this to the extent that you underdevelop your properties. Remember, too, that undeveloped properties can always be mortgaged—a handy way of obtaining a bit of ready cash, should the necessity arise.

The Bidder's Delight

The psychology of successful bidding is, essentially, to convince your opponent that the piece of property you want is awful, and the piece of property you *don't* want is wonderful. If you can manage to convince him, you'll find him most cooperative.

Never approach an auction with a poker face. Instead, let your face and actions indicate what you want him to think you're feeling. The attitude you show, of course, should generally be the opposite of what you really feel.

Suppose, for example, that Virginia Avenue is being auctioned. You already own all three Orange lots, and you really want to save your cash for building houses. But your opponent owns States Avenue, and you'd like to stop him from getting two properties in the same color group.

Frown slightly as the Bank announces that the property is being offered to the highest bidder. You can be a bit honest here, as you indicate that you should really be saving your money to develop your properties. But to buy a Maroon? Shudder delicately.

Glance covertly at your opponent's Title Deeds. Is that a Green card you see? Good gracious. He has a Green property, and he's wasting his time and money buying Maroons. Well, divide and conquer. Give him enough rope, and he'll hang himself.

If you've been talking aloud like this, your opponent may justifiably think you've gone mad. But with a bit of subtlety, you can shake his confidence just enough to make him hesitate. Then jump in with a sigh and magnanimously buy Virginia, almost as though you're doing him a favor.

Now, suppose Oriental is up for auction, and it's a property you *don't* want. Gasp slightly when a player refuses the chance to buy it, and lean forward as the Banker puts it up for auction. Is it really being made available? Are you really going to get the chance to get your hands on that valuable property? Wow!

The moment the bids open, make your offer—and offer high. Estimate, if you can, what your opponent was about to bid, and outbid him. He'll be annoyed, and probably raise your bid. Raise his. Let him raise you. Indicate your willingness to keep this up for awhile—but be careful not to raise each bid too much. Keep him in the running. Always remember that ultimately, when you have gotten him to make his highest offer, you're going to pull back and let him have the property. After all, you didn't want it in the first place. All you were after was to get your opponent to shell out as much money as possible in the purchase of a property you couldn't care less about.

Incidentally, if no one wants a property, buy it dirt cheap. You can always use it later, to trade or to mortgage. And if no one else offers a bid, make the Bank the lowest possible offer. Since you don't want the property anyway, why not try to buy it for a dollar or so. And while your opponents burst into either laughter or righteous indignation, push the Banker to close the bidding, and walk away with your deed.

The Railroad Offensive

The rent for a single Railroad is $25. But, unlike the color card properties, which double in value only when all of the Title Deeds in a group are owned, transportation charges increase with each additional Railroad you own.

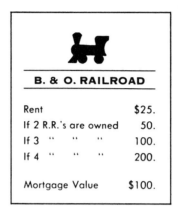

B. & O. RAILROAD

Rent	$25.
If 2 R.R.'s are owned	50.
If 3 " " "	100.
If 4 " " "	200.
Mortgage Value	$100.

A $25 fare is roughly equivalent to the rent on one Red or Yellow property with no buildings on it. Not bad for the beginning of the game.

A $200 fare is roughly equivalent to the rent on Boardwalk with one house, or either St. James or Tennessee with two houses. There is a difference, though: there are four Railroads, and if you own all of them, your opponent has a four times greater chance of landing on one of them than he has of landing on, say, Tennessee Avenue.

Statistically, however, because of other factors (e.g. the Chance card that says "Take a ride on the Reading Railroad"), three of the Railroads are among the most frequently landed-on properties. They are, respectively, in order of most frequent landings: the B&O Railroad, the Reading Railroad, and the Pennsylvania Railroad. The Short Line, which, after all, is only a nominal railroad anyway, has only a normal chance of being landed on.

Owning Railroads thus becomes most valuable at the beginning of the game. If you can, try to collect all of them by mid-game. That steady $200 can add up, and can keep your opponent mildly depleted of ready cash.

(Conversely, this is the time to prevent your opponent from gaining control of the Railroads.)

But the Railroads markedly lose their comparative value in the end-game, when property development is at its height. If you are involved in a rare game in which few if any houses are built, then by all means strive to get and keep all four Railroads.

But in a normal multiple dwelling end-game, the Railroads become good articles of trade. Offer one or two to your opponent (but not all four!) in return for a building lot that will give you control of a color group. Then get some houses up, fast.

The Utilities Folly

This section illustrates the error of buying a Utility late in the game or, worse yet, trading away another piece of property to get a second Utility.

Utilities are generally the worst investments on the board. If you own only one, the cost to your opponent is four times the amount shown on the dice. Since the highest number the dice can show is twelve, your maximum usage charge for one Utility is $48. This isn't too bad in the beginning of the game, but the comparative value drops as the game progresses.

If you own both the Electric Company and the Water Works, and your opponent lands on either one of these, he must pay you ten times the total shown on the dice, or a maximum of $120.

NOTE: The chances of throwing a twelve are one in thirty-six, not exceptionally high. Your opponent is much more likely to toss a five, six, seven, eight or nine (he has a two-thirds chance of tossing one of these). Your most probable usage charge, therefore, is only around $70.

Again, investing in Utilities at the beginning of the game isn't too awful, but as the game gets under way the best use to which you can put your Utilities is to:

a) mortgage them to give you needed cash, or

b) trade them for more profitable properties.

The Building Formation

When you buy houses and hotels from the Bank, you must place them evenly on all the properties of one color group. If you buy six houses and want to put them all on the Yellow properties, for instance, you would have to put two houses on each lot, like this:

Atlantic Avenue

Rent: $330

Ventnor Avenue

Rent: $330

Marvin Gardens

Rent: $360

Suppose you want to buy one more house. You may, since there may be a one-house difference on properties of the same color group, but on which lot should the extra house go? Obviously, on the lot that will be most profitable, and has the best chance of being landed on.

The easiest way to calculate which building lot would be most profitable with the extra house is simply to compare the different rents you could charge on each. With three houses:

Atlantic Avenue

Rent: $800

Ventnor Avenue

Rent: $800

Marvin Gardens

Rent: $850

If all other things are equal, then, you would put your extra house on Marvin Gardens.

If you take a good look at all the Title Deeds and compare them with their locations on the board, you will notice an interesting pattern. *In each color group, the farthest property from GO* (moving in a forward, clockwise direction, following the GO arrow) *has the highest rent for that group.*

In every case, the farthest property from GO has the highest rental within its color group. The first extra house you place on each color group

GO →	Mediterranean $10	Baltic $20	
GO →	Oriental $30	Vermont $30	Connecticut $40
GO →	St. Charles $50	States $50	Virginia $60
GO →	St. James $70	Tennessee $70	New York $80
GO →	Kentucky $90	Indiana $90	Illinois $100
GO →	Atlantic $110	Ventnor $110	Marvin Gardens $120
GO →	Pacific $130	North Carolina $130	Pennsylvania $150
GO →	Park Place $175	Boardwalk $200	

should always be placed on this farthest property. If you buy four houses to be placed on the Red group, then you would distribute the houses like this:

Kentucky   **Indiana**   **Illinois**

What if you buy another house for this group? Where do you put it? It doesn't really matter. There is only one case in which the placement of the second extra house is important. St. Charles Place, Illinois Avenue, and Boardwalk are the three building lots a player can be sent to by drawing a Chance card:

> Advance to St. Charles Place
> Advance to Illinois Avenue
> Advance token to Boardwalk

The probability of landing on these three properties is therefore higher than the probability of landing on other properties in those color groups.

Illinois Avenue and Boardwalk happen to be the farthest properties from GO in their respective color groups. Consequently, they are the most expensive properties in their groups, and your first extra house should be put on one of them. St. Charles Place is not the most expensive property in its group, but it does have a high probability of being landed on. When you are developing the Maroon properties, remember, therefore, to put the *second* extra house on St. Charles Place. For example, with one extra house:

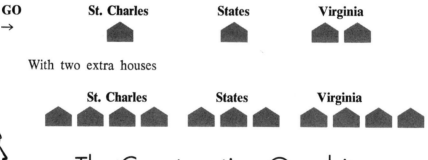

GO
→

St. Charles

States

Virginia

With two extra houses

St. Charles   **States**   **Virginia**

The Construction Gambit

Suppose you own two complete color groups, the Maroon and the Red, and you have already constructed one house on each of the Reds. You want to build three more houses. Do you put them on the Reds, or on the undeveloped Maroon properties?

Continue developing the Red group, since you've already begun building there. Remember, until you have at least three houses on each property, you're really operating at a loss. Keep adding houses to the color group you've begun building on until you have at least three houses on each property. If you need to do something drastic to raise the needed cash, you might even be justified in mortgaging the other property deeds in order to get these crucial houses built. Once you have them, you can relax and, if you wish, begin building up the second property group.

Suppose you have developed the Red properties to this point:

| Kentucky | Indiana | Illinois |

Now you pass GO and collect $200; immediately afterward your opponent is kind enough to land on Illinois and must pay you $750 rent. You now have a large amount of cash to spend on more houses, and the Bank has plenty of houses available. Where do you put them?

Your rent on Kentucky Avenue with two houses is $250. With a third house, it jumps to $700. The figures are the same for Indiana Avenue. At this point, with two houses apiece, your properties are still not bringing in a great profit. The great jump in rent from the second house to the third makes it important to get that third house on each property as quickly as possible. So you spend a total of $300 to construct the additional houses on Kentucky and Indiana. You still have $650 left from your windfall, in addition to the cash you had before, and you're still in a buying mood.

If you can add another $50 to your shopping money, go ahead and buy seven houses for the Maroon properties, and distribute them like this:

| St. Charles | States | Virginia |

It isn't quite the ideal of three houses on each property, but it's close. 111

The next time you purchase a building, be sure to put it on St. Charles Place (see The Building Formation above), and put the house after that on States Avenue.

Once you have your three houses on each property, you can continue to develop them at your leisure.

If you were cash-poor before all this happened, you would have had to reserve some of the $950 to cover future expenses. In that case, let's go back to your original holdings. You had no houses on the Maroon properties, and the following houses on the Red:

If you decide you can only spend around $500 right now, don't build any houses on the Maroon group. Put one additional house on Kentucky and Indiana, for a total cost of $300, and buy a fourth house for Illinois. As long as you are buying slowly, continue to develop this property group. The only time you would switch in the middle, and suddenly start developing another color group, is if you have enough money to construct three houses on each property all at once. Otherwise, finish building hotels on your first color group.

The Edifice Complex

There is another method of property control in Monopoly which is even more subtle than ownership of complete property groups, and if you can get it, or cooperate with certain players to cause it to happen, it can be one of the most valuable strategies in the game.

The Monopoly set comes equipped with twelve hotels and thirty-two houses. If the Bank runs out of houses or hotels, there is a building shortage; as long as it lasts, no one can erect any buildings on his or her property.

As you approach the end-game, most or all of the properties will have been bought, trades will have taken place, and there will be many complete color groups on the board. Players will have invested in houses, and some may be thinking of converting their houses to hotels. At this point in the game, the Bank frequently has a shortage of houses. Until players sell some houses back to the Bank, or return houses so that they can convert to hotels, no one will be able to construct more houses. And unless a player happens to have four houses standing on all the lots of one group, no one will be able to buy hotels, either. (You can only buy a hotel when there are four houses standing on all the building lots of that color group.)

Suppose there's a housing shortage, or very close to one, and you have four houses on each of the Orange building lots. On this one color group, then, you are holding twelve houses. You have some cash to invest, and you are thinking of converting your houses into hotels. Look around the board first. Does your opponent have a lot of cash to invest, and some expensive color groups just waiting to have houses built on them? If so, he's being badly hurt by the absence of available houses. The longer the housing shortage goes on, the more likely he is to land on someone else's expensive properties and have to pay out much of his money. The less money he has, the less dangerous he is to you.

But if you convert your houses to a hotel, you make those houses available to your now-wealthy opponent. Once he buys them, he stands a good chance of becoming even more wealthy, and every time you go around the board you must risk landing on expensive developed properties, instead of the relatively inexpensive undeveloped properties he now holds. At this point, it would be to your advantage, and probably to the advantage of your other opponents, to delay construction on hotels for awhile. Hold onto those houses. As long as you have them, in effect, you control the housing market, and this can prevent a potentially dangerous opponent from developing his properties.

If you already own some hotels, you can still use this strategy of rent control. If your opponent has come into sudden wealth and the Bank has a few houses available, it may be a good idea for you to break down one or more hotels and convert them into houses in order to create a housing shortage. Your reduced rents will still effectively drain your opponent's finances, and he will never get the chance to increase his own property values. You will make more money collecting rent for four houses, and paying out only small rents to your opponent, than you possibly could if you had a hotel and he had the chance to construct houses on his properties.

The Mortgage Morass

Mortgaging, remember, is a method of borrowing money from the Bank, in return for a 10 percent interest you will have to pay at the time you unmortgage a piece of property.

Q. What *can* be mortgaged?

A. Only undeveloped properties (properties which do *not* have houses or hotels standing on them). Buildings can *never* be mortgaged. They must be sold back to the Bank.

Q. When may you mortgage?

A. At any time during the game. Mortgage when you need money to pay rent, a fine, taxes, or simply to raise enough cash to buy a building or another piece of property.

Q. What *should* be mortgaged?

A. Well, it depends on what you have. The following list should give you an idea of the relative mortgageability of various properties. Depending upon how much you owe, and how much you own, mortgage your properties in approximately the following order:

Single Utilities

If you have *either* the Water Works or the Electric Company (but not both), this should probably be the first property to put in hock. In terms of income-producing value, one utility brings in an average rent of $28, with a rare maximum rent of $48 and an equally rare minimum of $8.

Single Building Lots

These would be part of a color group, of which you have only one: for example, Baltic Avenue, or Oriental, or Kentucky, or Boardwalk. Naturally, mortgage the cheapest properties you can get away with to leave yourself as many income-producing properties as possible. However, do bear in mind your opponent's proximity to your properties. If possible, avoid mortgaging something he's likely to land on in his next turn or two. Wherever possible, then, mortgage *behind* your opponent. Hold on to properties immediately in front of his token. If necessary, mortgage them next turn, when he's already passed them.

Remember, too, that certain properties are landed on much more frequently than others. If you have the choice of mortgaging either Ventnor or Illinois, mortgage Ventnor (even though it has a slightly higher rent). Remember the Chance card, "Advance to Illinois Avenue."

Pairs of Building Lots

If you own two out of three lots of a color group, and the third Title Deed of this group is still owned by the Bank (not by your opponent), consider your total financial position carefully. Is this cash shortage (the reason you need to mortgage something) only a temporary setback? Are you just strapped for a bit of ready cash? Are you, perhaps, cash-poor but property- (and buildings-)rich? Will you pass GO very soon and collect your $200 salary?

If your personal financial appraisal isn't too bad, try to avoid mortgaging this color pair. With a bit of good fortune, you may conceivably land on the third property (or be able to buy it at auction) and wind up with a complete building lot group. Not only will this automatically double the rental value of each of those properties, but it will also give you a ready-made opportunity to erect a house or two to quickly recoup your current losses.

Single Railroads

If it's the Short Line, treat it like a single Utility and mortgage it right away.

If it's any of the others, estimate your opponent's probability of landing on it, and, if possible, mortgage a Utility or a single building lot that has a lower rent, or a low probability of being landed on.

In general, though, consider all singly-owned Railroads as highly mortgageable.

Two Railroads

If one Railroad is the Short Line, mortgage it early. For one of the others, follow the above rule for mortgaging a single Railroad. Bear in mind, however, that when you own two Railroads, the rent to your opponent for landing on *either* of them is $50. Balance this against the rent you could get from a building lot when you decide which to mortgage first. Remember, if you mortgage only one of your two Railroads and your opponent lands on the other, he still must pay you $50.

Three or Four Railroads

Now you're getting into a higher income-producing bracket. With three Railroads, the rent for landing on any one of the three is $100. And if you own all four Railroads, it costs your opponent $200 each time his token takes a ride.

This is a good deal of steady income to be relinquished, and it requires some deeper consideration.

First, what is the stage of the game? If you're in either the early or midgame, with few buildings on the board, $100 or $200 means a great deal. If, however, your board has begun to look like a busy metropolis, the Railroad income might not be so important. (Unless all the buildings belong to your opponent!)

If you decide to mortgage Railroads, it may still be advantageous to hold on to one or two. Mortgage the Short Line first, and the Pennsylvania Railroad second. Hold on to the B&O and the Reading Railroad until last.

NOTE: If you've had to mortgage the three other Railroads but have managed to keep the B&O out of hock, remember that technically you still own the four Railroads. If your opponent foolishly lands on the B&O, he owes you $200.

Building Lot (Color) Groups

If you own an undeveloped color group, try not to mortgage any of the properties. The best way to make money (the way to make the most money) in the Monopoly world is to erect buildings. But you can't put a house on one property if another building lot from that same color group has been mortgaged.

If, regretfully, you must mortgage one or two lots from the same color group, remember that the rent for landing on the third lot is still doubled. In or out of mortgage, you still own the group.

NOTE: Mortgaging is a way to borrow money from the Bank. A mortgaged Title Deed should be turned, mortgage-side up, in front of you; you may mortgage at any time during the game. If you have a complete color group and mortgage only some of the properties from it, the higher group rent (two times as much for color building lots; $200 or eight times as much for Railroads; ten times the amount shown on the dice for a Utility) still applies to the remaining properties.

You may collect no rent on a property while it is mortgaged. No building lot can be mortgaged if it has one or more houses or hotels on it. First, the buildings must be *sold* back to the Bank.

The Profitable Loss

To be quite honest, there is no way to make a profit out of selling your houses or hotels back to the Bank. But you can sometimes minimize your loss. True, the Bank will only give you half the amount of money the buildings originally cost you, so monetarily it has to hurt. The idea is to make it hurt as little as possible.

First of all, if you *must* sell a building, think carefully about which building it should be. Most likely you have more than one, so choose the one whose loss will be least painful.

Wherever possible, try to retain three houses on each of your properties. If you have four houses on each of the Yellow lots and three houses on each of the Orange, sell the fourth house from a Yellow property. Don't, of course, sell the house from Marvin Gardens, since this is the highest-earning property of its group. (The extra house should always be on the highest-earning property of a color group, which is the farthest property from GO.)

Bearing this in mind, consider too where your opponents are on the board. Try to sell buildings *behind* your opponent, never in front of him. For instance, if your opponent's token is on the Pennsylvania Railroad and you have the choice of selling a house from States Avenue or from Tennesee, sell the house from States. Your opponent will have to circle the board before he gets the chance to land on the Maroon property group. But there is certainly a possibility that he may land on Tennessee during his coming turn, so hang onto that house if you can, at least until he's moved his token past it.

Suppose there is a building shortage. You have quite a bit of cash at the moment, but there are no houses to buy. If you don't invest the money soon, it will be used up paying rent to your opponent.

If you're desperate enough, you might be able to supply your own house. Suppose you had four houses on each of the Light Blue building lots. You purchased each house for $50; you could sell one back to the Bank for $25.

You also own the Yellow group, on which you've constructed two houses apiece. Your Yellow lots are losing money, but there's nothing you can do. The Bank has no more houses to sell.

Remember now, this is for emergencies only. O.K. Sell the house from Connecticut Avenue back to the Bank for $25. Now tell the Bank that you would like to buy the house it now has available, and erect it on Marvin Gardens. (The house will cost the normal purchase price of $150.)

It's a nice trick, but it has a catch. Once the Bank has the building, if more than one player wants to buy it the Bank must put it up for auction.

This could raise the price of the building considerably. Still, it is a way to get a building moved from one of your properties to another.

The Beggar's Offense

What do you do when you're cash-poor and you land on someone's expensive, well-developed property?

First of all, unless you're completely wiped out, don't let your opponent see that he's got you. Clench your toes if you must, but keep your face calm and your voice cheerful. Banter.

Do a fast total of your cash on hand, and figure out how much you still need. Keep your money beside you until you've done the rest of your manipulations—selling, mortgaging, trading. Do *not* pay your opponent in dribs and drabs.

"Here's $73.00. That means I still owe you . . . $682. Now, if I mortgage this . . . O.K., here's another $90. Now I'll sell . . . Hmm. How much have I paid you, so far?"

If your opponent has been obscenely rejoicing in your misfortune, he may not have kept track. And if he's a real Monopoly maven, he'll lie. Wouldn't you? So avoid tempting him. Do what you have to do to amass his rotten rent, and toss the whole amount to him in one fell swoop. With disdain. In small bills.

The Pecuniary Plunge

It's late in the game. The board is covered with houses and hotels. Atlantic Avenue, Ventnor, and Marvin Gardens are so covered with houses that you can't even see the yellow strip below them. It just looks like another row of Green properties. And they belong to your opponent, along with the real Greens.

Awhile ago, you had quite a bit of money, and you really wanted to do some building. You own the Light Blues, with two houses on each. A few turns ago, you traded away Illinois Avenue for Park Place, and now you own the Dark Blues, too. But the Bank had a building shortage, and for all this time you've been unable to buy a house.

Now your opponent has turned in four houses in order to construct a hotel on one of his properties. If you land on it, you'll be wiped out. For that matter, though, you're pretty close to being bankrupt anyway. But you do have nearly $300 in cash. Should you save it to pay the high rent you know you'll probably have to pay soon?

Oh, what the heck! You're probably going to lose anyway, and saving cash now isn't going to help you at all in the future. So splurge! Try a pecuniary plunge! Take your remaining money, and buy a house on the Boardwalk. You never know. . . .

The Bankruptcy Deferred

Good grief! A six? Oh, for . . . you threw a six?! Maybe you miscalculated. Move your token slowly. One. Two. Three. That's the game, fellas. A six. Marvin Gardens with a hotel. $1,200. Whew.

Slowly, you begin to remove the few houses you own so that you can sell them back to the Bank. The other players watch as you formally liquidate your holdings. Player Three, Marvin's owner, watches your every move. He even counts the money the Banker hands you for your houses. After all, the money will soon be turned over to him—he's not about to be cheated.

As you gather up your Title Deeds, his eyes gleam. He's about to get the Maroon color group from you, and Pacific Avenue as well. You've held on to Pacific throughout the game to keep him from getting the Greens. He already owns North Carolina and Pennsylvania. And he has more than enough cash to put buildings on them immediately. The other players have begun to fidget.

And there's your solution! Offer to sell some of your properties to Player Two; he's got a bit of cash, and he's got even more to lose if Player

Three acquires your properties and starts developing them. Player Two is, naturally, delighted by the suggestion. Player Three calls foul.

NOTE: You owe Player Three $1,200. You don't have that much cash, and you cannot transfer buildings to another player so you have sold your houses back to the Bank. You still don't have enough cash. Your only other assets are your properties, so your creditor naturally demands them as his own.

Technically, you are obligated to pay your creditor the amount of money you owe him, if you can. And if you can't, you must return your buildings to the Bank, turn over "all that you have of value" to him, and "retire from the game." In other words, you must give your creditor all your properties, mortgaged or not.

But your primary obligation must be to try to pay your creditor in full, and making a sale to Player Two might permit you to do just that. If Player Two gives you enough money to enable you to pay off your *complete* debt, you may agree to the trade. But if Player Two will only offer you a small amount of money for your properties, and you will still be unable to pay Player Three's hotel bill even after the trading is completed, then you may not go through with the trade. You may not deliberately reduce the value of your assets in order to reduce the profits your properties would bring to your creditor.

NOTE: You do not have to sell to the highest bidder. Suppose Player Two offers you $1,300—enough to pay your debt to Player Three and keep you in the game, nominally. Player Four might offer $1,500, and may even be willing to throw in the Electric Company, just because he's a nice guy.

You may sell your properties to either player.

Now Player Three himself gets into the act. He'd prefer to bankrupt you entirely, but since he can't do that anymore, he'll settle for mortally wounding you, and gaining an additional edge over the others. Player Three, your creditor, offers the best deal yet: he'll settle for Pacific, States, and Virginia Avenues, and he'll give you the Water Works and $500. This would settle your debt, leave you still in the game with a little cash, and you'd now own the Water Works and St. Charles Place. He, on the other hand, would now own all of the Green properties, and two pieces of the Maroon color group.

Of the three offers, this is the best one. Should you take it? That depends on how you feel about the eventual outcome of the game (as well as how you are feeling, at this moment, about the individual players). With any of the deals, you stand virtually no chance of winning—but there is always the hope that your opponents might land on one another's properties and wipe each other out. If you become exceedingly lucky, and if the game continues long enough, there is the very odd chance that you could ultimately make a comeback.

The probabilities are against you, though. One of your opponents will most likely be the eventual winner. What you do now could influence which one it will be; and this factor could, if you wish, help you make your decision. Your only restriction is that you must be able to pay your creditor, in full (or on lesser terms that he may agree to), at the end of your trade. If that is not to your liking either, you can wash your hands of the whole mess and go bankrupt. (Remember that this will, by default, give your creditor the ammunition of your properties.)

Beat the Cheat

Monopoly is a game of good, wholesome fun, and it's really deplorable that some people find the need to cheat at it. But, like shoplifting, cheating seems to be an overwhelming impulse that sometimes gets the best of even otherwise law-abiding people. After all, winning does mean so much.

The best way to avoid being cheated is to be aware of various cheating practices. If you know what someone might try, you can be on the lookout for it. Awareness is the best defense, or something. Anyway, here are a few of the most common cheating tactics.

1. Look for a telltale smirk if your opponent draws a Chance card, holds it close to him, and reads: "Your building and loan matures. Collect $150."

If in doubt, ask to inspect the card. You may find that it really reads "Pay poor tax of $15."

2. If you have to leave the room in the midst of a game, be certain to do a quick count of your money, property deeds, and buildings. When you return, make sure nothing is missing.

3. Watch out for the overly efficient player who supposedly knows the board so well that he can see at a glance how many squares to move his token without actually counting. It's easy to estimate ten squares, but often players jump their tokens around the board without actually touching every space in between. They toss off careless remarks like: "Eight. Let's see . . . that puts me here, on Illinois. It's mine. You go." Or "Twelve. By now, I can tell just by glancing at the board. Twelve should put me here, on Free Parking. You go."

Check your opponent by counting the squares to see if he has really put his token onto the proper square. Maybe, instead of Free Parking, he should have landed on New York Avenue with a hotel. And maybe you own New York Avenue.

4. When your token lands on your opponent's property with one or more houses on it, his eye must flick down his Title Deed to see how much rent you should pay. Be sure that his eye does not flick one line too many. He might just quote you the price for four houses, when he has only three houses standing on the lot.

5. And speaking of houses, once a color group has several houses on each lot, it can tend to look a bit jumbled. If your opponent has an extra house on one or two of his properties, be careful that they stay where they were originally constructed. For example, suppose your opponent owns the Maroon color group, and has built two houses on St. Charles Place, three houses on Virginia Avenue, and two houses on States Avenue. St. Charles and States are separated from one another; the Electric Company is in between. But States and Virginia are right next to one another. Now, suppose you land on States Avenue, which should have only two houses on it. If your opponent was a bit clumsy, accidentally or on purpose, he might have man-

aged to slide the third house from Virginia over so that it looks as though it is a third house on States Avenue. You could wind up paying a higher rent if you don't watch out.

6. Sometimes two tokens happen to land on the same square, or even quite near one another. Your opponent, who owns one of these tokens, may throw the dice and realize that if he moves his token the indicated number of spaces, he'll owe you a lot of money. So he "accidentally" picks up the wrong token and moves it, instead. Or he picks up his own token, moves it a few squares, and then "gets confused" in his count and has to begin all over again. "Where was I," he'll say bewilderedly, scratching his head with one hand as he lifts his token with the other and moves it backward to its starting square. But does he? Keep track of the board so that you can remember where his token was standing. If he moves it back to a wrong square, and then recounts his moves from there, he might happen to land one square before or after your highly developed property, to his delight and your detriment.

7. Try to keep track of the status of everyone's properties, and beware of the player who habitually picks up his mortgaged Title Deed to "study it." He's just liable to put it down with the unmortgaged side showing.

These are not earth shaking acts of sabotage, but they can certainly affect the course of the game. To avoid having someone cheat you, just follow the Boy Scout motto: be prepared.

Epilogue: How to Deal with Tantrums

Sooner or later, if you play Monopoly often enough, you'll run into an opponent who has a tendency to throw tantrums. If you make a study of the phenomenon, you'll notice that, for some odd reason, tantrums rarely if ever occur when a person is winning. So a tantrum can be a clue that your opponent is losing. Or thinks he is. Or, at the very least, that he thinks he's gotten the worst end of a deal.

Tantrums vary from person to person, and even within the same individual from time to time. There are, however, certain general characteristics and symptoms which will help you to identify a common tantrum.

Guidelines for Identifying a Tantrum

a) the victim's face tends to grow red and flushed. Some victims grow white and pale. Some victims flicker.

b) the victim's voice tends to rise in pitch, sometimes reaching a D above high C.

c) the voice tends to increase markedly in volume. Sometimes this is preceded by a short period of excessively soft, clipped speech.

d) the hands tend to clench, and sometimes flail about wildly. This can cause inconvenience and even possible damage to players sitting nearby, but is most particularly hazardous to the player who is then in the role of creditor.

e) in advanced cases, profuse moisture may be exuded by the victim, sometimes in the form of excessive perspiration, sometimes as a salty liquid emitted from the corners of the eyes.

Tantrums rarely erupt spontaneously. Most often, they are preceded by warning signs. If you learn to recognize them, you can often predict when a tantrum is about to occur.

Warning Signs

a) a tantrum is often preceded by a protestation. In sudden cases, this may be only one word, such as: "Hey!"

b) the victim's facial muscles may contract, producing an appearance of tenseness, even of a grimace.

c) the victim may speak very slowly and deliberately, enunciating each word in a precise and deliberate manner. The voice may grow unnaturally soft, even become a whisper.

d) the eyes may grow momentarily glassy, then darken as the brows knit above them.

e) a low rumbling may be emitted from the victim's chest.

If you are faced with a fullblown tantrum, there is little you can do to relieve it. The most constructive thing you can do is to try to minimize further shock to the victim until the attack has had a chance to run its full course. If your opponent suddenly flies into a tantrum after landing on Pennsylvania Avenue with a hotel, sit quietly while he rages, but watch carefully as he converts his buildings and properties into the cash necessary to pay you the required rent. People in the midst of tantrums tend to have difficulty with the processes of elementary mathematics. This disability sometimes communicates itself to others in the game. This is a time for utmost discretion, however, in pointing out such errors. If your Banker makes a mistake computing the amount of money he should give to your opponent on the sale of his hotel, don't suggest that he practice his multiplication tables after work each day for a week, and certainly don't offer to help drill him on them. Just mention casually that you think the Bank should have given your opponent five times the price of a house, divided by two—which is $50 less than the Banker actually paid him. Then smile helpfully at your opponent. This should help his tantrum.

Be ready to supply technical information concerning the rules. In the midst of a tantrum, for instance, your opponent may mistakenly sell a hotel back to the Bank and elect to retain three houses on that property. Do your opponent the kindness to point out that the build evenly rule requires him to sell *two* hotels in return for four houses on each of the two properties. He will appreciate your thoughtful attention to detail.

The most difficult tantrums to deal with are those that result from multiple dealing. Suppose Player Two lands on Player Three's property, which has a hotel standing on it. Player Two cannot afford the rent, and is about to go bankrupt. Rather than deprive Player Two of the fun of continued play, you step in and offer to buy Player Two's properties for $500 more than the sum of the debt. This would enable Player Two to pay off his or her debt, and would give him or her an additional $500 spending money to continue the game. As it happens, it would also give you Player Two's Light Blue and Red groups plus the Green North Carolina Avenue. Player Three, by coincidence, owns the other two Greens.

In such a situation, Player Three could conceivably lapse into a tantrum. He might querulously insist that Player Two landed on *his* property, which makes *him* the creditor and heir to his or her total holdings. Pointing out the bankruptcy deferred strategy might sooth him, but conceivably it might not. His condition could be worsened if it happens that he and Player Two are married. In this case, it is often appropriate to mumble something about getting the coffee and retire to the kitchen until you hear the door slam. If it is not your kitchen, you can take this opportunity to remember that you have an exceedingly early plane to catch tomorrow morning.

As you can see, tantrums, while momentarily unpleasant, can nonetheless be dealt with successfully if you remember to keep calm, smile but don't smirk, and avert your eyes discreetly if your opponent begins to froth.

Above all, don't panic.

Appendix:
Property Development Tables

The tables that follow allow you to see at a glance how much it will cost to build houses and hotels on the color group(s) you control. The tables incorporate the build-evenly rule which is, of course, the only legal building alternative you have. As it will bring you most profit, *they also assume you will put your first extra house and first hotel on the most expensive property in each group*—Connecticut Avenue in the Light Blue group, Virginia Avenue in the Maroon group, New York Avenue in the Orange group, and so on. The most remunerative property in each group is indicated by an asterisk (*) on the tables. In all cases of three-property groups, the two less-expensive lots cost the same amount and charge the same lower rent.

The percentage of profit is indicated wherever property development is equal; that is, when there are the same number of houses and hotels on all the properties of the color group. The percentage is based on the cumulative development cost of the entire color group up to that point, the total rent of all properties at that stage, the percent of return for the color group and the number of properties in the group.

A quick check of the chart for each property group will show you at a glance what your investments on that group will bring you. And since the aim of the game is profit, it's always nice to know what you're getting for your money.

PURPLE PROPERTY GROUP

	Purchase Price	Rent	Mortgage Rate	10% Mortgage Interest
Mediterranean Avenue	$60	$2	$30	$3
*Baltic Avenue	$60	$4	$30	$3

Houses cost $50 each
Hotels cost $250 each ($50 + 4 houses)

| Property Development | Cumulative Development Costs | Rental Income: | | Percentage of Profit |
		*Baltic Avenue	Mediterranean Avenue	
Property Group	$120	$ 8	$ 4	5%
1 House	170	20	4	
2 Houses	220	20	10	6.8%
3 Houses	270	60	10	
4 Houses	320	60	30	14%
5 Houses	370	180	30	
6 Houses	420	180	90	32.2%
7 Houses	470	320	90	
8 Houses	520	320	160	46.2%
1 Hotel + 4 Houses	570	450	160	
2 Hotels	620	450	250	56.5%

LIGHT BLUE PROPERTY GROUP

	Purchase Price	Rent	Mortgage Rate	10% Mortgage Interest
Oriental Avenue	$100	$6	$50	$5
Vermont Avenue	$100	$6	$50	$5
***Connecticut Avenue**	$120	$8	$60	$6

Houses cost $50 each

Hotels cost $250 each ($50 + 4 houses)

Property Development	Cumulative Development Costs	Rental Income: *Connecticut Avenue	Oriental Avenue Vermont Avenue	Percentage of Profit
Property group	$ 320	$ 16	$ 12	4.2%
1 House	370	40	12	
2 Houses	420	40	30 or 12	
3 Houses	470	40	30	7.9%
4 Houses	520	100	30	
5 Houses	570	100	90 or 30	
6 Houses	620	100	90	15.0%
7 Houses	670	300	90	
8 Houses	720	300	270 or 90	
9 Houses	770	300	270	36.4%
10 Houses	820	450	270	
11 Houses	870	450	400 or 270	
12 Houses	920	450	400	45.3%
1 Hotel + 8 Houses	970	600	400	
2 Hotels + 4 Houses	1020	600	550 or 400	
3 Hotels	1070	600	550	53 %

MAROON PROPERTY GROUP

	Purchase Price	Rent	Mortgage Rate	10% Mortgage Interest
St. Charles Place	$140	$10	$70	$7
States Avenue	$140	$10	$70	$7
*Virginia Avenue	$160	$12	$80	$8

Houses cost $100 each
Hotels cost $500 each ($100 + 4 houses)

Property Development	Cumulative Development Costs	*Virginia Avenue	Rental Income: St. Charles Place States Avenue	Percentage of Profit
Property Group	$ 440	$ 24	$ 20	5%
1 House	540	60	20	
2 Houses	640	60	50 or 20	
3 Houses	740	60	50	7%
4 Houses	840	180	50	
5 Houses	940	180	150 or 50	
6 Houses	1040	180	150	15%
7 Houses	1140	500	150	
8 Houses	1240	500	450 or 150	
9 Houses	1340	500	450	35%
10 Houses	1440	700	450	
11 Houses	1540	700	625 or 450	
12 Houses	1640	700	625	39.6%
1 Hotel + 8 Houses	1740	900	625	
2 Hotels + 4 Houses	1840	900	750 or 625	
3 Hotels	1940	900	750	41.2%

ORANGE PROPERTY GROUP

	Purchase Price	Rent	Mortgage Rate	10% Mortgage Interest
St. James Place	$180	$14	$ 90	$ 9
Tennessee Avenue	$180	$14	$ 90	$ 9
***New York Avenue**	$200	$16	$100	$10

Houses cost $100 each
Hotels cost $500 each ($100 + 4 houses)

Property Development	Cumulative Development Costs	Rental Income:	St. James Place	Percentage of Profit
		*New York Avenue	Tennessee Avenue	
Property Group	$ 560	$ 32	$ 28	5.2%
1 House	660	80	28	
2 Houses	760	80	70 or 28	
3 Houses	860	80	70	8.5%
4 Houses	960	220	70	
5 Houses	1060	220	200 or 70	
6 Houses	1160	220	200	17.8%
7 Houses	1260	600	200	
8 Houses	1360	600	550 or 200	
9 Houses	1460	600	550	38.8%
10 Houses	1560	800	550	
11 Houses	1660	800	750 or 550	
12 Houses	1760	800	750	43.6%
1 Hotel + 8 Houses	1860	1000	750	
2 Hotels + 4 Houses	1960	1000	950 or 750	
3 Hotels	2060	1000	950	46.9%

RED PROPERTY GROUP

	Purchase Price	Rent	Mortgage Rate	10% Mortgage Interest
Kentucky Avenue	$220	$18	$110	$11
Indiana Avenue	$220	$18	$110	$11
*Illinois Avenue	$240	$20	$120	$12

Houses cost $150 each

Hotels cost $750 each ($150 + 4 houses)

Property Development	Cumulative Development Costs	Rental Income: *Illinois Avenue	Rental Income: Kentucky Avenue Indiana Avenue	Percentage of Profit
Property Group	$ 680	$ 40	$ 36	5.5%
1 House	830	100	36	
2 Houses	980	100	90 or 36	
3 Houses	1130	100	90	8.3%
4 Houses	1280	300	90	
5 Houses	1430	300	250 or 90	
6 Houses	1580	300	250	16.9%
7 Houses	1730	750	250	
8 Houses	1880	750	700 or 250	
9 Houses	2030	750	700	35.3%
10 Houses	2180	925	700	
11 Houses	2330	925	875 or 700	
12 Houses	2480	925	875	36.0%
1 Hotel + 8 Houses	2630	1100	875	
2 Hotels + 4 Houses	2780	1100	1050 or 875	
3 Hotels	2930	1100	1050	36.4%

133

YELLOW PROPERTY GROUP

	Purchase Price	Rent	Mortgage Rate	10% Mortgage Interest
Atlantic Avenue	$260	$22	$130	$13
Ventnor Avenue	$260	$22	$130	$13
*Marvin Gardens	$280	$24	$140	$14

Houses cost $150 each
Hotels cost $750 each ($150 + 4 houses)

Property Development	Cumulative Development Costs	Rental Income: *Marvin Gardens	Atlantic Avenue Ventnor Avenue	Percentage of Profit
Property Group	$ 800	$ 48	$ 44	5.6%
1 House	950	120	44	
2 Houses	1100	120	110 or 44	
3 Houses	1250	120	110	9%
4 Houses	1400	360	110	
5 Houses	1550	360	330 or 110	
6 Houses	1700	360	330	20%
7 Houses	1850	850	330	
8 Houses	2000	850	800 or 330	
9 Houses	2150	850	800	38%
10 Houses	2300	1025	800	
11 Houses	2450	1025	975 or 800	
12 Houses	2600	1025	975	38%
1 Hotel + 8 Houses	2750	1200	975	
2 Hotels + 4 Houses	2900	1200	1150 or 975	
3 Hotels	3050	1200	1150	38.3%

GREEN PROPERTY GROUP

	Purchase Price	Rent	Mortgage Rate	10% Mortgage Interest
Pacific Avenue	$300	$26	$150	$15
North Carolina Avenue	$300	$26	$150	$15
***Pennsylvania Avenue**	$320	$28	$160	$16

Houses cost $200 each

Hotels cost $1000 each ($200 + 4 houses)

Property Development	**Cumulative Development Costs**	**Rental Income:** *Pennsylvania Avenue	**Pacific Avenue North Carolina Avenue**	**Percentage of Profit**
Property Group	$ 920	$ 56	$ 52	5.8%
1 House	1120	150	52	
2 Houses	1320	150	130 or 52	
3 Houses	1520	150	130	9 %
4 Houses	1720	450	130	
5 Houses	1920	450	390 or 130	
6 Houses	2120	450	390	19.3%
7 Houses	2320	1000	390	
8 Houses	2520	1000	900 or 390	
9 Houses	2720	1000	900	34.3%
10 Houses	2920	1200	900	
11 Houses	3120	1200	1100 or 900	
12 Houses	3320	1200	1100	34.1%
1 Hotel + 8 Houses	3520	1400	1100	
2 Hotels + 4 Houses	3720	1400	1275 or 1100	
3 Hotels	3920	1400	1275	33.6%

DARK BLUE PROPERTY GROUP

	Purchase Price	Rent	Mortgage Rate	10% Mortgage Interest
Park Place	$350	$35	$175	$18
***Boardwalk**	$400	$50	$200	$20

Houses cost $200 each
Hotels cost $1000 each ($200 + 4 houses)

Property Development	Cumulative Development Costs	Rental Income: *Boardwalk	Park Place	Percentage of Profit
Property Group	$ 750	$ 100	$ 70	11.3%
1 House	950	200	70	
2 Houses	1150	200	175	16.3%
3 Houses	1350	600	175	
4 Houses	1550	600	500	35.5%
5 Houses	1750	1400	500	
6 Houses	1950	1400	1100	64.1%
7 Houses	2150	1700	1100	
8 Houses	2350	1700	1300	63.8%
1 Hotel + 4 Houses	2550	2000	1300	
2 Hotels	2750	2000	1500	63.6%

Property Desirability Index

The Property Desirability Index that appears on the following page expresses, in one figure, the percentage of return on investment, and the probability of landing on the properties of each color group. The result indicates the true value of each group at every level of building development, *and enables you to compare the color groups to see how the return on your investment varies according to how many buildings you construct, and where you place them.*

Most color groups show a continuous, but variable increase in profit as additional houses or hotels are built on them. Note that the biggest jump usually occurs at the third house: most properties become truly profitable at this point.

Occasionally, "expensive" properties show a retrograde motion when they are highly developed. The Greens are the best example of this. With three houses, their desirability factor is 2.9878. With four houses, the factor decreases to 2.9736, and with a hotel it drops to 2.9256. This doesn't mean that you're losing money; it just means that while building costs are increasing at the same rate (the fourth house costs the same as the third), rent for that fourth house is increasing in a lesser proportion, so the fourth house is *relatively* less profitable than the third. If you have three houses on the Reds and three on the Greens, and enough cash to buy one more house for all the lots of either color group, the PDI indicates that the fourth house should be placed on the Red properties.

I would like to thank Professor Irvin R. Hentzel, Mathematics Department, Iowa State University, for his data on the probability of landing on each square.

Property Desirability Index

	1 House	2 Houses	3 Houses	4 Houses	1 Hotel
Purple	.3283	.6765	1.5472	2.2203	2.7200
Light Blue	.5460	1.1582	2.7999	3.4872	4.0778
Maroon	.7128	1.3077	2.9584	3.3675	3.5048
Orange	.8422	1.7586	3.8325	4.2991	4.6272
Red	.8038	1.6472	3.4322	3.4940	3.5368
Yellow	.8054	1.7773	3.3750	3.3905	3.3989
Green	.7824	1.6833	2.9878	2.9736	2.9256
Dark Blue	.8844	1.9292	3.4942	3.5289	3.4765

Parker Brothers'
Official Monopoly Rules

Object . . . The object of the game is to become the wealthiest player through buying, renting and selling property.

Equipment . . . The equipment consists of a board, 2 dice, tokens, 32 houses and 12 hotels. There are Chance and Community Chest cards, a Title Deed card for each property and play money.

Preparation . . . Place the board on a table and put the Chance and Community Chest cards face-down on their allotted spaces on the board. Each player chooses one token to represent him on his travels around the board.

Each player is given $1500 divided as follows: 2 each of $500's, $100's and $50's; 6-$20's; 5 each of $10's, $5's and $1's.

All remaining money and other equipment go to the Bank.

Banker . . . Select as Banker a player who will also make a good Auctioneer. If the Banker plays in the game, he must keep his personal funds separate from those of the Bank. When more than five persons play, the Banker may elect to act only as Banker and Auctioneer.

The Bank . . . Besides the Bank's money, the Bank holds the Title Deed cards and houses and hotels prior to purchase and use by the players. The Bank pays salaries and bonuses. It sells and auctions properties and hands out their proper Title Deed cards; it sells houses and hotels to the players and loans money when required on mortgages.

The Bank collects all taxes, fines, loans and interest, and the price of all properties which it sells and auctions.

The Bank never "goes broke". If the Bank runs out of money it may issue as much more as may be needed by merely writing on any ordinary paper.

The Play . . . Starting with the Banker, each player in turn throws the dice. The player with the highest total starts the play. He places his token on the corner marked "GO", throws the 2 dice and moves his token in the direction of the arrow the number of spaces indicated by the dice. After he has completed his play, the turn to play passes to the left. The tokens remain on the spaces occupied and proceed from that point on the player's next turn. Two or more tokens may rest on the same space at the same time.

According to the space which his token reaches, a player may be entitled to buy real estate or other properties,—or be obliged to pay rent, pay taxes, draw a Chance or Community Chest card, "Go to Jail", etc.

If a player throws doubles he moves his token as usual the sum of the two dice and is subject to any privileges or penalties pertaining to the space on which he lands. Retaining the dice, he throws again and moves his token as before. If a player throws doubles three times in succession, he moves his token immediately to the space marked "In Jail" (see JAIL).

"Go" . . . Each time a player's token lands on or passes over "GO", whether by throw of the dice or by drawing a card, the Banker pays him $200 salary.

However, $200 is paid only once each time around the board. If a player, passing "GO" on the throw of the dice, lands 2 spaces beyond it on "Community Chest", or 7 spaces beyond it on "Chance", and draws the card "Advance to GO", he collects $200 for passing "GO" the first time and another $200 for reaching it the second time by instructions on the card.

Buying Property . . . Whenever a player lands on an unowned property he may buy that property from the Bank at its printed price. He receives the Title Deed card showing ownership and places it face-up in front of him.

If he does not wish to buy the property it is sold at auction by the Banker to the highest bidder. The buyer pays to the Bank the amount of the bid in cash and receives the Title Deed card for that property. Any player, including the one who declined the option of buying it at the printed price, may bid. Bidding may start at any price.

Paying Rent . . . When a player lands on property owned by another player the owner collects rent from him in accordance with the list printed on the Title Deed card applying to it.

If the property is mortgaged, no rent can be collected. When a property is mortgaged its Title Deed card is placed face-down in front of the owner.

It is an advantage to hold all the Title Deeds in a color-group (i.e.: Boardwalk and Park Place,—or Connecticut, Vermont and Oriental Avenues) because the owner may then charge double rent for unimproved properties in that color-group. This rule applies to unmortgaged properties even if another property in that color-group is mortgaged.

It is even more of an advantage to have houses or hotels on properties because rents are much higher than for unimproved properties.

The owner may not collect his rent if he fails to ask for it before the second player following throws the dice.

"Chance" and "Community Chest" . . . When a player lands on either of these spaces he takes the top card from the deck indicated, follows the instructions and returns the card face-down to the bottom of the deck.

The "Get Out of Jail Free" card is held until used and then returned to the bottom of the deck. If the player who draws it does not wish to use it he may sell it, at any time, to another player at a price agreeable to both.

"Income Tax" . . . When a player lands on "Income Tax" he has two options: he may estimate his tax at $200 and pay the Bank, or he may pay 10% of his total worth to the Bank. His total worth is all his cash on hand, printed prices of mortgaged and unmortgaged properties and cost price of all buildings he owns.

The player must decide which option he will take *before* he adds up his total worth.

Jail . . . A player lands in Jail when . . . (1.) his token lands on the space marked "Go to Jail"; (2.) he draws a card marked "Go to Jail"; (3.) he throws doubles three times in succession.

When a player is sent to Jail he cannot collect $200 salary in that move since, regardless of where his token is on the board, he must move it directly into Jail. A player's turn ends when he is sent to Jail.

If a player is not "sent to Jail" but in the ordinary course of play lands on that space, he is "Just Visiting", incurs no penalty, and moves ahead in the usual manner on his next turn.

A player gets out of Jail by . . . (1.) throwing doubles on any of his next three turns. (If he succeeds in doing this he immediately moves forward the number of spaces shown by his doubles throw. Even though he has thrown doubles he *does not* take another turn.); (2.) using the "Get Out of Jail Free" card if he has it; (3.) purchasing the "Get Out of Jail Free" card from another player and playing it; (4.) paying a fine of $50 before he rolls the dice on either of his next two turns.

If the player does not throw doubles by his third turn he *must pay* the $50 fine. He then gets out of Jail and immediately moves forward the number of spaces shown by his throw.

Even though he is in Jail, a player may buy or sell property, buy or sell houses and hotels and collect rents.

Free Parking . . . A player landing on this space does not receive any money, property or reward of any kind. This is just a "free" resting place.

Houses . . . When a player owns all the properties in a color-group he may buy houses from the Bank and erect them on those properties.

If he buys one house, he may put it on any one of those properties. The next house he buys must be erected on one of the unimproved properties of this or any other complete color-group he may own.

The price he must pay the Bank for each house is shown on his Title Deed card for the property on which he erects the house.

The owner can still collect double rent from an opponent who lands on the unimproved properties of his complete color-group.

Following the above rules, a player may buy and erect at any time as many houses as his judgment and financial standing will allow. *But he must build evenly* (i.e.: he cannot erect more than one house on any one property of any color-group until he has built one house on every property of that group. He may then begin on the second row of houses, and so on, up to a limit of four houses to a property. For example, he cannot build three houses on one property if he has only one house on another property of that group).

As a player builds evenly, he must also break down evenly if he sells houses back to the Bank (see SELLING PROPERTY).

Hotels . . . When a player has four houses on each property of a complete color-group, he may buy a hotel from the Bank and erect it on any property of that color-group. He returns the four houses from that property to the Bank and pays the price for the hotel as shown on the Title Deed card. Only one hotel may be erected on any one property.

Building Shortage . . . When the Bank has no houses to sell, players wishing to build must wait for some player to turn back or to sell his houses to the Bank before building. If there are a limited number of houses and hotels available, and two or more players wish to buy more than the Bank has, the houses or hotels must be sold at auction to the highest bidder.

Selling Property . . . Unimproved properties, railroads and utilities (but not buildings) may be sold to any player as a private transaction for any amount that the owner can get. However, no property can be sold to another player if buildings are standing on any properties of that color-group. Any buildings so located must be sold back to the Bank before the owner can sell any property of that color-group.

Houses and hotels may be sold back to the Bank at any time for *one-half* the price paid for them.

All houses on one color-group must be sold one by one, evenly, in reverse of the manner in which they were erected.

All hotels on one color-group may be sold at once. Or they may be sold one *house* at a time (one hotel equals five houses), evenly, in reverse of the manner in which they were erected.

Mortgages . . . Unimproved properties can be mortgaged through the Bank at any time. Before an improved property can be mortgaged all the buildings on all the properties of its color-group must be sold back to the Bank at half price. The mortgage value is printed on each Title Deed card.

No rent can be collected on mortgaged properties or utilities, but rent can be collected on unmortgaged properties in the same group.

In order to lift the mortgage, the owner must pay the Bank the amount of the mortgage *plus* 10% interest. When all the properties of a color-group are no longer mortgaged the owner may begin to buy back houses at full price.

The player who mortgages property retains possession of it and no other player may secure it by lifting the mortgage from the Bank. However, the owner may sell this mortgaged property to another player at any agreed price. The new owner may lift the mortgage at once, if he wishes, by paying off the mortgage plus 10% interest to the Bank. If he does not lift the mortgage at once he must pay the Bank 10% interest when he buys the property and if he lifts the mortgage later he must pay an *additional* 10% interest as well as the amount of the mortgage to the Bank.

Bankruptcy . . . A player is bankrupt when he owes more than he can pay either to another player or to the Bank. If his debt is to another player, he must turn over to that player all that he has of value and retire from the game. In making this settlement, if he owns houses or hotels, he must return these to the Bank in exchange for money to the extent of one-half the amount paid for them and this cash is given to the creditor. If he has mortgaged property he also turns this property over to his creditor but the new owner must at once pay the Bank the amount of interest on the loan, which is 10% of the value of the property. After the new owner does this, he may, at his option, pay the principal or hold the property until some later turn at which time he may lift the mortgage. If he holds property in this way until a later turn, he must pay the interest again when he lifts the mortgage.

Should a player owe the Bank, instead of another player, more than he can pay (because of taxes or penalties) even by selling his buildings and mortgaging property, he must turn over all his assets to the Bank. In this case, the Bank immediately sells by auction all property so taken, except buildings. A bankrupt player must immediately retire from the game. The last player left in the game wins.

Miscellaneous . . . Money can only be loaned to a player by the Bank and then only by mortgaging property. No player may borrow from or lend money to another player.

RULES for a SHORT GAME (60 to 90 minutes of fun)

There are three differences in rules for this "Short Game".

1. During **Preparation** for play the Banker shuffles the pack of Title Deed cards. The pack is then cut by the player at his left and the Banker deals, one at a time, two Title Deed cards to each player (including himself if he both plays and acts as Banker). Players receiving Title Deed cards must immediately pay the Bank the printed price of each of the two properties thus acquired. The play then commences as in the regular game.

2. In this short game it is only necessary to have three houses (instead of four) on each lot of a complete color-group before the player may buy a hotel.

Rent received for a hotel remains the same as in the regular game.

The turn-in value of a hotel is still one- 143

half the purchase price, which in this game is one house less than in the regular game.

3. End of Game. The first player to go bankrupt retires from the game as in the regular game. However, when the second bankruptcy occurs the game ends. Play immediately ceases with the bankrupt player turning over to his creditor all that he has of value, including buildings and any other properties—whether the creditor happens to be a rival player or the Bank.

Each remaining player then values his property: (1.) cash on hand; (2.) lots, utilities and railroads owned by him at the price printed on the board; (3.) any mortgaged property owned by him at one-half price printed on the board; (4.) houses, valued at purchase price; (5.) hotels, valued at the purchase price including the value of the three houses turned in.

RICHEST PLAYER WINS!

ANOTHER GOOD SHORT GAME

Time Limit Game . . . Before starting, agree upon a definite hour of termination richest player then winning. Before starting the game, Title Deed cards are shuffled and cut, and Banker deals two Title Deeds to each player. Players immediately pay the Bank the price of property dealt to them.